HEAR

THE VOICE OF GOD

BY

WALLACE H. HEFLIN, JR.

HEAR THE VOICE OF GOD

All Scripture references are from the Authorized
King James Version of the Bible, unless otherwise
noted.

Published by:

McDougal Publishing

P.O. Box 3595
Hagerstown, MD 21742-3595

ISBN 1-884369-36-7

Printed in the United States of America
For Worldwide Distribution

CONTENTS

Introduction 5

**Part I: The Importance of Hearing the Voice of
God** 11
1. God's Invitation To You 13
2. How It Affected My Ministry 17
3. Why We Should Expect It 33
4. What It Will Do For Us 45

Part II: How God Speaks to His People 57
5. Through His Word 59
6. Through Dreams and Visions 75
7. Through Prophecy 87
8. Through An Audible Voice 93
9. Through A Still, Small Voice 105
10. Through Desire 113
11. Through Mature Believers 117
12. In the Way He Can Best Reach You 123

**Part III: Hindrances to Hearing the Voice of
God** 127
13. Sin, Lack of Spirituality 129
14. Wrong Teachings and Wrong Influences 133

15. Not Really Wanting to Hear 139

Part IV: Hearing the Voice of God and How It
     Affects Ministry 151
16. Hearing and the Gift of Prophecy 153
17. Hearing and Faith For Finances 157
18. Hearing and the Missionary Vision 163
19. Hearing and Being A Watchman 167
20. Hearing and Spiritual Leadership 175

Part V: Developing A Sensitivity to the Voice
     of God 183
21. The Importance of Prayer and Fasting 185
22. Walking Softly Before the Lord 189
23. Learning Through the Offering 195
24. Declaring What You Hear 203

My Prayer For Your Hearing 207

INTRODUCTION

As we move ever closer to the culminating moments of time, one of the greatest needs of the Church is Divine guidance. As leaders of the Church and as everyday members, as well, we desperately need to hear the voice of God. Why this has become such a difficult point for many is sometimes hard for me to understand. It should not be so.

God is our Father, and we must be in constant communication with Him. Wouldn't it be terrible to live in a house where the father never spoke to his children? Wouldn't it be terrible to live in a home where you had to try to read your father's mind, to know what he was thinking, or what he expected of you? What a terrible way to live! Believe me, that is not the way our Heavenly Father does things. He loves us and wants the very best for us. Therefore He is willing to give us very explicit instructions in life — if we are willing to listen and obey.

But even for those who want to hear and want to obey there seem to be many obstacles: What does God's voice sound like? How can we recognize it? How can we know that we are not moving by impulse or even being led astray by the Devil? These are commonly asked questions among both new and older Christians, reflecting a general ignorance on the subject of hearing the voice of God. In fact, no teaching is more desperately needed today.

The concept of hearing God's voice has always been real to me. My parents talked to God all the years we were growing up, and they expected us to talk to God. They expected to get answers from God, and they expected us to get answers from God. But even in a worldly sense, I have a hard time understanding why some discount this truth and insist that it is difficult or impossible to hear and understand the voice of God.

Before I gave my heart to the Lord and became a preacher, I was a salesman. In the later fifties, before being drafted into the army, I lived and worked in New England for a time; and, because I was from the South, my friends nicknamed me "Rebel."

The Army sent me to Korea for two years, and when I got back I wondered if all my friends had forgotten me. As soon as I got a chance, I picked up a phone and called my old buddy Phil.

"Hello, Phil," I said, without identifying myself. "How are you?"

Without any hesitation on his part, he replied, "Well, hello, Rebel. How ya doin'?"

I have never forgotten that experience. The man hadn't heard my voice for two long years, that's seven hundred and thirty consecutive days, yet he immediately recognized my voice on the telephone. Now, if Phil, a good friend, knew my voice, I think we, as children of God, should know the voice of our Heavenly Father and of our Savior and Lord, Jesus Christ. He is much more than a friend.

Why shouldn't we know the voice of God? Why shouldn't we understand what He is saying to us? Why shouldn't we be able to tell what comes from Him and what is not from Him? Why shouldn't we be able to recognize the voice of the Devil or the voice of flesh speaking to us?

We must know, for we cannot afford to be stepping outside of the will of God. We cannot afford to be stabbing in the dark; for time is too short, and there is too much at stake. We are dealing with the precious things of eternity.

As we shall see, hearing the voice of God was an expected experience in Bible days and all the great men and women of the Bible personally communed with God. Then, down through the ages, somehow the understanding of how easy it is to hear from God was lost so that those who did hear from Heaven were thought to be so special that they were honored as saints of the Church.

Still today, very few Christians expect to hear the voice of God. This is sad, because we can say with a certainly that it is more important for us to be able to hear the voice of God now than it ever has been in history.

We are living in the closing days of time, in the culmination of God's work on the earth, in the period of preparation of the Bride of Christ for the coming Wedding of the Lamb. Therefore, hearing the voice of God is imperative. If we fail to cultivate the ability to hear God's voice, we will limit what He can do for us in these last days. How will we know His will for each step we take? How can we move at His direction if we cannot know His direction?

Let us lay again the biblical foundations for hearing the voice of God, examine the things that might prevent us from doing so, and see how we can each start developing the sensitivity necessary in this critical hour to *Hear the Voice of God.*

Wallace Heflin, Jr.
September, 1996

The Lord God hath given me the tongue of the learned, that I should know how to speak a word in season to him that is weary: he wakeneth morning by morning, he wakeneth mine ear to hear as the learned. The Lord God hath opened mine ear, and I was not rebellious, neither turned away back.

Isaiah 50:4-5

PART I

THE IMPORTANCE OF HEARING THE VOICE OF GOD

CHAPTER ONE

GOD'S INVITATION TO YOU

Behold, I stand at the door, and knock: if any man hear my voice, and open the door, I will come in to him, and will sup with him, and he with me.

Revelation 3:20

There can be no question. God is still speaking to His people, and He is extending a personal invitation to you today to hear His voice. He speaks through His Word; He speaks through dreams and visions; He speaks through prophecy and other gifts of the Spirit; He speaks in an audible voice; He speaks through a still, small voice; He speaks through placing His desires in our heart; and He speaks to us through mature believers.

We can be hindered from hearing His voice by flagrant sin or a general lack of spirituality, or by wrong teachings or wrong influences; but the thing that hinders us most is an unwillingness to hear, for fear that we will not want to do what God is telling us. We flee from God, not the other way around. He speaks to those who are willing to hear and obey.

Hearing the voice of God is critical to the ministry of the prophet; for the prophet simply repeats what he hears God saying. Hearing the voice of God is critical to the life of faith, for the life of faith is simply doing what God tells you to do, expecting Him to pick up the tab. Hearing the voice of God is critical to the missionary vision, for if we cannot hear His voice, where shall we go? When? With whom?

Hearing the voice of God is critical to the ministry of the mature believer to become a watchman who guards others from danger and warns when it approaches. Hearing the voice of God is critical to leadership in the Church because men and women have always been willing to work with those who are in contact with Heaven and have God's favor evident upon their lives.

Prayer and fasting, walking softly before the Lord, practicing hearing the voice of God through our giving and being bold to begin declaring what God reveals to us for others are all part of the way we can develop a sensitivity to God's voice.

God is concerned about every area of our lives. He is interested in our health, in our relationships, and in our bank account and will speak to you in all those areas. It is to your benefit to get God involved in the intimate details of your everyday existence, because too many times when we take things into our own hands we make a mess of them.

If business people could hear the voice of God, they would never make a bad investment, never buy something that will not sell, never put their money into something that would not reap an abundant return. People who listen carefully to God are successful and prosperous people.

Hearing the voice of God should be just as natural as saying GOOD MORNING to your spouse or children. Although hearing God's voice is a special experience, every believer should have it regularly. Although we should never take it for granted, we should expect it and contend for it on a regular basis. God wants you to hear His voice, to know His will and understand His purposes.

When you encounter problems in life, you need to know who is creating those problems. Is it God who is trying to stop you because what you are doing is not His will? Or is it the Devil who is trying to stop you because you are on the right road?

Never make a major decision in life without first getting in contact with God. It's too dangerous, and you can't afford to play with your future. My mother always said, "Don't change trains in a tunnel. It's dark, you might catch the wrong one." None of us wants to make a mistake, we must be careful.

God knows how to open doors — if you can hear His voice and step through them. God knows how to supply your need — if you are where He wants you to be at the moment He wants you to be there. God knows how to save you money — if you will listen to Him. God can help you buy the right automobile. He knows just the model that will give you the best service at the best possible cost.

As you become willing to allow God to move as He wills, things will get better and better for you in the days ahead, the glory of God will fall upon your household, and your life will be filled with great excitement. Let go, and let God work.

The best way I know to hear the voice and to know the mind of God is to get neutral on the subject, and that's not easy. Your flesh has its own ideas about what it does or does not want to do. You must be ready to go or ready to stay, ready to act now or ready to wait for a future time, ready to speak or ready to be silent. Then, when you hear the voice of God, you won't be in danger of applying your own interpretation to what He says.

Living by hearing the voice of God is the most exciting life anyone could imagine. It's a constant thrill! It is exciting to know that our God is so mindful of the details of your everyday life and so desires that you have life's best that He shows you each step to take in the way.

Most people need several weeks to pray about an invitation, and by the time they discover that it is God's will, the opportunity has passed. When the Spirit of God speaks to you, what is there to pray about? Developing a sensitivity of hearing toward God will ensure that your life is enriched, that you move on to greater things.

Chapter Two

How It Affected My Ministry

*Behold, I have set before thee an open door, and
no man can shut it: for thou hast ... kept my word.*
Revelation 3:8

The message of this book is, for me, a very personal one. Hearing the voice of God has meant all
the difference in my personal life and in my ministry, enabling me to go places I could not have
otherwise gone and to do things that I could not have
otherwise done. Because I have been willing to hear
and obey His voice, God has opened unusual doors
of opportunity to me. Let me share with you just a
few examples:

Ministry to An African Queen

Once, when I was crossing the Sea of Galilee with
a group we had gathered to visit the Middle East,
the King and Queen of Nigeria were on the same
boat. They were dressed very regally, but God told
me that the Queen was ill and needed my prayers. I

went to her side and told her what God had showed me. "My arm is hurting me so badly I can hardly sit still," she replied. I laid hands on her, and the power of God hit her so that she let out a scream. "It's gone! It's gone!" she shouted.

She had seemed like such a quiet and conservative person, but God had done a miracle for her, and she was happy about it. You never know what God has in store for you. This miracle has been repeated over and over again in places around the world.

MINISTRY TO THE DEAF AND DUMB AND THE SICK

In one of my tent meetings, a man came with his wife and two children. They were all deaf and dumb. Not one of them could hear, and not one of them could speak. I knew that God was going to deliver them, but I felt it was important which one I ministered to first, for the healing of one would give faith to all the rest.

It seemed to me that it might be respectful to pray for the mother and father first, but God said 'no' and told me to pray for the boy first. When God delivered the boy, he got so excited that it caused new faith to rise up in the girl. Then, when God opened the ears of the girl and she began to talk, I expected that seeing the two children healed would give faith to the parents so that they could be healed too. When I turned to them, however, they declined to be prayed for. They had been deaf so long they did not want to hear. Then I understood what God had done. If I had tried to pray for them first, their unbelief could have robbed the children of their miracle.

God knows exactly how to do His work. We must trust Him and listen carefully to His instructions. Many times, in our services, we miss what God wants us to do because we have our own preconceived order. For instance, it has been the tradition of Pentecostal churches for many years to have prayer lines for the sick and suffering at the close of the service, after the preaching. Often, however, I have heard the Spirit of God saying to the congregation earlier in the service, "I have come to heal. I have come to give you miracles." How can God do miracles if we don't give Him an opportunity to do them?

The Church is His. The Word is His. The ministry is His. Every meeting is His. Let Him run it as He wants to. He knows what He is doing. Let Him do it.

When we open up to God and give Him opportunity to work, we are always the winners.

AUSTRALIAN DOORS OPEN TO US

IN 1973, after attending the World Pentecostal Conference in Seoul, Korea, Mother and I stopped off in Hong Kong on our way home and were invited to preach in a local church there. At the close of the service, the pastor said to me, "If God sends you back to Hong Kong, I want you to conduct a revival meeting in this church."

"If I come back, it will be just for you," I assured him.

The first Sunday that we were home the Holy Ghost spoke to us in the service and said, "Retrace your steps." Brother Jack Chappell agreed to accompany me and I sent a telegraph to that Chinese pastor saying, "God spoke to me to return," and I outlined for him the two weeks that I felt I could dedicate to Hong Kong.

We also planned to go to Australia to speak in Sydney and Melbourne, two cities we had previously visited, and then we were to go on to New Zealand, before retuning home. While we were praying one morning in Hong Kong the Lord spoke to me in that still, small voice and said, "Change your tickets, and go to Perth, and go to Adelaide." I didn't know a soul in either of those cities, but I was sure that I had heard from God.

I said to Brother Chappell, "God just told me to change our tickets and go to Perth and Adelaide, instead." Getting there proved to be difficult. Many flights had been canceled due to the oil embargo and existing planes were very full.

We flew from Hong Kong to the Philippines, then from Manila to Singapore and into Indonesia to get a connection into Australia. When we arrived in

Djakarta, however, we were told that the flight to Australia was full and, worse, that there would be no available seats for several days.

Although I had nothing against staying in Indonesia, and we had valid visas for that country, I felt that we needed to go on. The agent insisted that some airline personnel were being bumped from the flight because there were too many full-fare passengers and assured me that there was no way we could get on.

I told Brother Chappell that we should pray, and we began walking through the airport, talking to God. I had a New Testament in my pocket and when I opened it with the prayer, "God, give me a scripture. Should we go or not?" My finger landed on a scripture that said, "Go." I said, "Brother Chappell, you and I are going to get on that plane."

I went back to the ticket agent and said, "You know, the Lord just told me ..."

He said, "Preacher, I told you that plane was full."

I said, "God just told me that I'm going to get on that plane."

He said, "The plane is full, but if it will help you any, we'll close out the boarding list a little early. If anyone is late, you can take their seats." That day two Pentecostal preachers got the last two seats on a plane headed for Australia.

We arrived in Perth at five o'clock in the morning. While we were in the Philippines, someone had told us about an American missionary that was in Perth, so we intended to go see him, but it was too early, so we got a hotel room.

We had very little money with us. Before we had left Hong Kong, God had spoken to me to send a large portion of what I had to our camp in South America. So, here we were living in a hotel in Australia, knowing no one, and with only $125 to our name.

A little later that day, when we came out of the hotel, we passed a car rental place, and God told me to rent a car. On the chance that the missionary might have a car and would help us, and we could save a little, we passed up the car rental and caught a bus and a taxi to take us across town to find the missionary. When we reached the place the American missionary was living, sure enough, there was a car in his driveway.

We visited with the brother for about an hour and were ready to go back into town. We were surprised when he said, "I'm very sorry I can't take you to town. I've just blown the motor in my car." Both of us wished at that moment that we had obeyed the voice of God and rented a car.

Since that first brother couldn't help us, God sent us to another brother. He had a small business, as well as his church. Two months before God had told him that He would send two men from the east to strengthen his hand. On the Sunday before we arrived he had called his people to three days of fasting, believing that God was about to do something new for them. We met on Wednesday.

When we met that day, he knew, within a very short time, that we were the two men he had been looking for. We ministered to him and his office staff, as for the next forty-five minutes the phones did not ring even once. The glory of God fell in that office.

We stayed seven weeks in Perth and had a city-wide meeting in which three or four hundred Catholic priests and nuns were baptized in the Holy Ghost. What a joy it was to look out over the congregation and see all those sisters in their white habits rejoicing before God. The revival in the Catholic Church in Australia continues even today. As you can imagine, all of our financial needs were met miraculously.

We were thankful to God that we heard His voice saying to us, "Change your tickets and go to Perth." He was not finished with us yet. He had said "Perth" and "Adelaide."

A lady in Perth, when she heard that we were going on to Adelaide, gave us the name of her son who was living there. So when we arrived in Adelaide, we called him. He was married to a pastor's daughter and arranged for us to have lunch with his father-in-law the following day. The man was over hundreds of churches. He was very conservative and felt it necessary to tell us that people did not dance in his church and just what he allowed and did not allow from visiting ministers.

He felt that we had probably come at a bad time of the year, since Christmas was nearing and that we would have few open doors. When we asked about the Catholics in Adelaide, he told us that the two groups, Catholics and Pentecostals, were not on speaking terms. We sensed that we would not be ministering for that group.

When we got out into our rented car, we decided to go looking for some hungry Catholics. We found a phone book and looked up convents. The nearest one turned out to belong to the Carmelites and within minutes we were there. We spoke with the Mother Superior and found the group to be very hungry for the things of God. She invited us to come back on Thursday night to minister to the sisters concerning the baptism of the Holy Ghost.

On Thursday night we spent two hours telling the nuns about the baptism of the Holy Ghost. After our meeting, the Mother Superior told us of a couple who were about to be married. The woman was Spirit-filled, but the young man was not and was attending an Episcopalian school. He was dissatisfied with his experience, however, and she suggested that we go by and pray for the two of them.

It was already ten o'clock by the time we got to

the house the couple were painting and fixing up, getting ready for their new life together. Within a few moments God had baptized the man with the Holy Ghost and he was rejoicing in the Lord.

I got a call early the next morning from the Mother Superior, asking me to go by and pray for her mother and aunt who were leaving town later that day. For quite some time, her mother had been seriously ill and under a doctor's care.

We had contacted another local Pentecostal group and were expecting two pastors to come by and show us around the town. When we got in the car, we asked them if they would mind taking time to make this visit, and they agreed to accompany us. When we laid hands on those two Catholic women, God not only healed them, but He filled them with the Holy Ghost, as well.

Before we left that place the two men said to us, "Would you mind visiting a woman who is on a dialysis machine? Her kidneys have stopped working, and she needs prayer." We went with them to lay hands on that woman. The power of God came upon her and began to heal those kidneys. We never did get in any sight-seeing that day.

Our two minister friends didn't know quite what to think of us. We were, for one thing, the noisiest people they had ever met in their lives. Something strange, however, had happened in their church on Sunday which caused them not to reject us outrightly. The Lord had spoken to them that He was sending two angels their way. They were not sure that we were angels, but they felt they had to "take a chance" on us. So they began to open doors for us in the city. We stayed seven weeks in Adelaide and preached in every one of the churches belonging to that particular denomination. God did unusual things. One example:

God got hold of the hearts of a Methodist couple, and over a period of two weeks they personally brought fifty of their friends and relatives to be blessed. Each of the friends and relatives, they told us later, either got saved, healed, or filled with the Holy Ghost.

God used those meetings in Adelaide to open Australia to us, and we have been back there many times. Many years passed before I got to New Zealand, but God knows where He needs us and when. Be willing to hear His voice and obey.

SPIRITUAL FIESTA IN THE PHILIPPINES

In the early seventies, God told us that He wanted to do something in the Philippines that would impact all of Asia and be heard in the whole world. It did not seem like a propitious time, as Filipino college students were rioting in the streets, but God knows what He is doing. Several of us heard His voice and went there to join others who were believing God for revival, and it came.

My sister Ruth arrived in the Philippines some weeks before my father and me and worked with Brother Harold McDougal and his missionaries and Bible students. Their Bible school building had been destroyed in a typhoon, and the Lord had told them that there was a purpose. He wanted them in the capital city where they could prepare for revival.

All Bible school activities were curtailed, and for many weeks the entire group spent each day learning how to worship the Lord. Little did they know that they would be the instruments of revival to carry the fire of God's Spirit to every province of that nation and, later, to other nations. They were just moving one step at a time, as they heard the voice of God; and God was preparing to do the work.

I got there just in time. The very large charismatic movement that exists in the Philippines today began on January the 21st, 1971, in the Quezon City Municipal Stadium. Many of those who had heard of the visions and revelations received over a short period of time by those involved in this movement were skeptical and were not excited to take part. After all, who were these people? And why would God use them? It is true that those who were involved in planning the historic Spiritual Fiesta in the Philippines were simple people who had a listening ear.

Very little money was available to do all that God

was speaking, but before long we found ourselves on national television. Because of the rioting that had been occurring regularly throughout the major cities of that country, people were staying home, and they were watching television. Our audience for those live telecasts from the stadium was estimated at 550,000.

The people watching saw God doing miracles. They saw people slain in the Spirit. They saw people weeping before God and getting saved. They saw sick men and women being healed by the power of God. On the very first night of the crusade they saw a man on crutches throw down those crutches and run across the platform. The impact was enormous.

The most powerful impact of the televised meetings was upon the leadership of the Catholic Church. Why so many of them happened to be watching those telecasts no one can say for sure, but what they saw deeply impressed them, and they soon began calling, asking our people to come and pray for them. They wanted to have immediate and positive answers to their prayers, as they had seen God doing for us.

It didn't just happen. In a meeting of Catholic Church officials in the days immediately following the crusade, a respected leader had said, "Our people will never be the same after having seen these Pentecostals on television. We have two choices: either we lose our people to them, or we can have

Pentecost in the Church." The decision was made, and before long we were all busy laying hands on priests, in their monasteries and schools, and on nuns, in their convents and places of service.

No one has been able to keep count of those blessed though this great revival. At one time the number 5 million was being used. Later we heard 10 million or 15 million. The total is probably more, since it has continued for so many years and intensified.

The original crusades were conducted in four major cities. Afterward, not many knew Wallace Heflin, but everyone had heard of the impact of the Spiritual Fiesta, the Pentecostal Outpouring, and everyone knew that God had visited the Philippines.

Two years after the original Spiritual Fiesta Crusades, a Time Magazine article noted the large number of Filipinos who had been swept up in the revival and the large number of nations reached by Filipino missionaries in the aftermath of that revival. Now a new history book, being used in Filipino schools, gives an entire last chapter to The Great Revival and the way that revival has changed the Philippines and the surrounding nations.

It all happened because someone heard the voice of God and was willing to go — before others had thought of the Philippines as a missionary nation at all.

Again, in these days, God's Spirit desires to take

us out into new areas, to lead us in new paths, to take us in ways that we have never walked before; and we can only do that as we hear His voice and learn to walk in His ways.

DON'T GO

The *stays* of God are just as important as His *go's*. If we can hear God's voice telling us to go somewhere to work for Him, we can also hear His voice telling us not to go and even to cancel our plans. One year I was planning to go to Australia and preach for several weeks in a tent. The idea was very exciting to me. Then, for no apparent reason, I lost all desire to go.

God sent a brother from England to minister in our church. After he preached, he asked for those who had a desire to go to India to come forward. He wanted to pray for them. He asked for those who had a desire to minister in England. Then he asked for those who had a desire to minister in Australia. Four or five people lined up to get prayed for, but I felt absolutely nothing. While he prayed for those who had a desire to go, I sat behind him on the platform. For some reason, I had lost all desire for the trip.

I didn't understand what it was all about, but I knew that I would be out of the will of God to get on a flight going to Australia, when He had lifted the burden and the desire from my heart. When I got back home that night, I went to my office and sat down at my desk to dial Australia and give the news to the pastor who had invited me. As I was preparing to dial the phone, it rang, and it was a call from Australia. It was not the man I had intended to call, but another brother. "I hear you're coming," he said. "I want you to come to my church."

I said, "I'm sorry that you are the first to know, but I'm not coming. God has lifted the burden from me; and, for some reason, I actually feel a restraint. I cannot come just now."

I called those who had invited me and explained my reasons for not going, and I didn't go. I feel that strongly about God's leading.

Where would I be without the leading of God's Spirit, without being able to hear the voice of God on a daily basis? I really can't imagine it.

CHAPTER THREE

WHY WE SHOULD EXPECT IT

*And they heard the voice of the Lord God walking
in the garden in the cool of the day:*

Genesis 3:8

Expecting to hear the voice of God is based upon God's very act of creation. He created man because He longed for fellowship. He needed someone with whom He could communicate. And, after creating Adam and Eve, God did communicate with them on a regular basis: *"they heard the voice of the Lord God."*

God enjoyed these moments of intimacy just as much as Adam and Eve did. They were just as important to Him as they were to man and to woman. In the same way that Adam and Eve looked forward to intimate times of fellowship with God and set aside anything else that might intrude on those moments, God looked forward to seeing Adam and Eve, to hearing what they had to say and to sharing what was on His heart with them.

In a great sense then, hearing the voice of God is

the very reason for our existence. We were created for communion with God. That is why God placed us here on the earth.

When, over time, man's intimate relationship with God came to an end, it was not God who broke it off. How could He? This was His heart's desire in creating man in the first place. How could He voluntarily end the sweet fellowship He had enjoyed so much? The intimacy ended only when sin crept into man's heart and caused him to be ashamed to talk with God and, instead, to hide himself from God. The same verse that tells of the intimacy God and man enjoyed also tells of its ultimate destruction:

> *And they heard the voice of the Lord God walking in the garden in the cool of the day: and Adam and his wife hid themselves from the presence of the Lord God amongst the trees of the garden.*
> Genesis 3:8

As long as sin was not allowed to intrude upon their relationship, God kept regular appointments with Adam and Eve and conversed freely with them. When sin made its ugly appearance, however, all that changed — not because God decided it should, but because man willfully withdrew from his Creator and hid himself from the presence of God.

When Adam and Eve hid, God was still there

walking around looking for them, walking around just as before, expecting to meet them, expecting to exchange intimacies with them. They could hear Him walking. As God, He was aware of all that had transpired between them and the Serpent. As God, He knew all that was in their hearts. Still, He came to meet with them. Still He longed for fellowship with them.

It was man who withdrew from God, not the other way around. Just because man had sinned didn't mean that God had changed. In fact, He had not changed; His desire for fellowship with Adam and Eve had not changed; and His will for their lives had not changed. Something had changed, and had changed drastically, but it was not God.

Sin separated man from God, not because God stopped loving man, but because sin made man self-conscious and uncomfortable in the presence of his Creator. Sin made man feel unworthy to even be in God's presence, let alone hear God's voice, feel God's touch, and be intimate with Him. Sin didn't change God, but it did change man. God still wanted to speak with Adam, but Adam was afraid to talk with God. So *Adam and his wife hid themselves from the presence of the Lord God."*

That day began a tragic chapter in the history of mankind, a history of rebellion and all its tragic consequences, a history that continues to be written today. But God still has not changed, and His desire for communion with those who love Him and choose His way is still in effect. He still makes His regular visits, still walks up and down, searching for those who will not hide from Him, who will open their hearts to His love and hear Him out.

When we love God and want to be obedient to Him, when our desire is to do all that He has spoken to us, all that He has called us to do, every barrier to fellowship with Him is removed; and nothing should prevent us from hearing His voice and feeling His touch on a regular basis. This is God's express will for each and every believer.

Hearing the voice of God did not cease with New Testament times. If you are God's child, you need to hear your Father's voice. He said:

> *For as many as are led by the Spirit of God, they*
> *are the sons of God.* Romans 8:14

How can you be *"led by the Spirit of God"* if you cannot hear and know what God is saying to you? It simply can't be done.

Those of us who love Him have a great desire to hear His voice, and we have every right to feel that way. He is everything to us. He means more to us than any other person alive, more than any family member, any friend or any acquaintance. Why, then, should we be deprived of His presence? We have a right to be near Him. We have a right to feel His caress. We have a right to hear His voice. And no one can deny us that right.

Our generation has decided that God has forgotten His creation and, for the most part, refuses to be contacted. This is not a new idea. In each generation, men have decided that communicating with God was impossible, or that God didn't even care what happened to man. The prophets were forced to declare that it was not so:

> *Behold, the Lord's hand is not shortened, that it cannot save; neither his ear heavy, that it cannot hear:* Isaiah 59:1

Jesus Himself came to show mankind that God had not forgotten His creation. He stated very emphatically:

> *My sheep hear my voice, and I know them, and they follow me: And I give unto them eternal life; and they shall never perish, neither shall any man pluck them out of my hand.* John 10:27-28

A good shepherd cares for his sheep, communicating to them when it is time to go out to pasture, when it is time to find the still waters, and when it is time to find shelter from the storm. The sheep follow him because they know him and trust him. They hear his voice and recognize it as one who cares for them and always helps them find what they need.

Jesus portrayed Himself as the Good Shepherd, ready to do anything for His sheep. This analogy of believers as sheep and God as our Shepherd is used throughout scripture:

> *All we like sheep have gone astray; we have turned every one to his own way; and the Lord hath laid on him the iniquity of us all.* Isaiah 53:6

> *For he is our God; and we are the people of his pasture, and the sheep of his hand.* Psalms 95:7

On another occasion, David, a shepherd in his own right, wrote:

> *The Lord is my shepherd; I shall not want. He maketh me to lie down in green pastures: he leadeth me beside the still waters. He restoreth my soul: he leadeth me in the paths of righteousness for his name's sake. Yea, though I walk through the valley of the shadow of death, I will fear no evil: for thou art with me; thy rod and thy staff they comfort me. Thou preparest a table before me in the presence of mine enemies: thou anointest my head with oil; my cup Runneth over. Surely goodness and mercy shall follow me all the days of my life: and I will dwell in the house of the Lord for ever.* Psalms 23:1-6

Why We Should Expect It

Jesus used the teaching of shepherd and sheep over and over. He said:

> *Verily, verily, I say unto you, He that entereth not by the door into the sheepfold, but climbeth up some other way, the same is a thief and a robber. But he that entereth in by the door is the shepherd of the sheep. To him the porter openeth; and the sheep hear his voice: and he calleth his own sheep by name, and leadeth them out. And when he putteth forth his own sheep, he goeth before them, and the sheep follow him: for they know his voice. And a stranger will they not follow, but will flee from him: for they know not the voice of strangers.* John 10:1-5

The Lord is our Shepherd, and He expects us to hear His voice and to follow Him. What could be more plain?

This concept of hearing the voice of God became common in the time of the Early Church. Men and women who loved God expected to hear from Him — in detail. When Saul of Tarsus was converted on the road to Damascus, God spoke to Ananias, a disciple of that city, to go minister to His new son:

> *And there was a certain disciple at Damascus, named Ananias; and to him said the Lord in a vision, Ananias. And he said, Behold, I am here,*

Hear the Voice of God

Lord. And the Lord said unto him, Arise, and go into the street which is called Straight, and inquire in the house of Judas for one called Saul, of Tarsus: for, behold, he prayeth, And hath seen in a vision a man named Ananias coming in, and putting his hand on him, that he might receive his sight. Acts 9:10-12

God's instructions to Ananias, who had been asking God to use him to bless others, were specific and detailed. God told him what street to go to, what house to go to, what name to ask for and what to do when he found the man he was looking for. When Ananias heard the name "Saul of Tarsus," he was frightened and wanted to back out of his offer. He knew Saul to be a man who was severely persecuting the Church and had heard that Saul was even then on his way to Damascus with letters authorizing him to do similar damage in their city. But God showed Ananias His plan for Saul, a plan that would take him to many nations to bless many people. The knowledge that Saul had been blinded was also comforting to Ananias. Surely the man could do no further harm. So, Ananias obeyed the Lord and went to find this man named Saul.

At the same time that God was showing Ananias the details of His plan, He was also working on the other end. Saul, a new Christian, was receiving a detailed vision that showed him exactly what was

Why We Should Expect It

about to happen. He saw a man coming to pray for him and knew what the man's name was and how he would proceed. So God used a relatively unknown disciple of Damascus to heal the future Apostle Paul, to filled him with the Holy Ghost, and to set his soul on fire through a prophecy which showed him *"how great things he must suffer"* for the Lord's sake.

This is exactly how God wants to do it. Whether we are new believers, those who have known the Lord for some time, or those who have known the Lord for many years, His will is to speak to each of us, in the way He knows best, and lead us into His perfect plan for our lives. Hearing the voice of God should be as natural as breathing for the child of God.

God sent three men from Caesarea to the house where Peter was visiting in Joppa. As the men were nearing the place, Peter was having a vision in which he saw a great sheet let down out of Heaven and all sorts of animals caught up in it. The vision didn't seem to make sense to him because the voice he heard said, "Rise, Peter, kill and eat," but the animals he had seen in the net were "unclean," those that God had told His people not to eat. When he questioned the Lord about this, the Lord said, "Don't call common or unclean what I have cleansed." This was repeated three times, but still Peter wasn't sure what it all meant.

He was soon to find out what it meant when he

learned that three men were at the gate seeking him and that they had been sent by someone named Cornelius, an Italian who was desirous of hearing more about the ways of the Lord. Peter wondered if it was right for him to be ministering to those who had, for centuries, been considered "common" or "unclean," and as he thought on this, the meaning of the vision became clear to him. Whether he understood it before leaving Joppa or if the full meaning of the vision became clear to him only as he was on his way to Caesarea we don't know. But whatever the case, everything was all right by the time Peter arrived at the house of Cornelius and revival came to the Gentiles. That's the way God will speak to us today — if we trust Him.

John's Revelation is so powerful because it is not something that he imagined or thought up, but something he actually experienced. He heard the voice of God:

> *I was in the Spirit on the Lord's day, and heard behind me a great voice, as of a trumpet, Saying, I am Alpha and Omega, the first and the last: and, What thou seest, write in a book, and send it unto the seven churches which are in Asia; unto Ephesus, and unto Smyrna, and unto Pergamos, and unto Thyatira, and unto Sardis, and unto Philadelphia, and unto Laodicea. And I turned to see*

Why We Should Expect It

the voice that spake with me. And being turned, I
saw seven golden candlesticks;

Revelation 1:10-12

This experience of hearing the voice of God was common to all of the apostles of the first-century Church and has been repeated over and over again since then by those believers who contended for it, both men and women, and both clergy and laymen.

Hearing the voice of God should not be unusual. Not hearing the voice of God should be the unusual thing. To those who, for some reason or other, could not hear His voice, the Lord pleaded through John, the Revelator: *"He that hath an ear, let him hear what the Spirit saith unto the churches."* It is possible, or He would not have pleaded with us to hear.

Although it is possible, however, not everyone who has ears can hear God's voice. For some reason, many are crippled in this regard. They, therefore, are doomed to advance on logic or experience or tradition or consensus and can never be sure that they are wholly following the Lord. I feel sorry for these people.

Knowing that God is willing and eager to walk and talk with us twenty-four hours a day, to speak with us while we are on our job, to speak with us while we are on our way to and from work, to speak to us first thing in the morning and in the still hours of the night, I, for one, refuse to settle for less.

And when I hear Christians saying things like,

"I'm not sure whether that's God or not," or "I'm afraid that might be my flesh and not God," it bothers me. We simply cannot continue in this way. We simply must cultivate a sensitivity to His voice. There is too much at stake. Perhaps if we understand what hearing the voice of God will do for us it will motivate us all to work harder on this spiritual ability.

CHAPTER FOUR

WHAT IT WILL DO FOR US

*Obey, I beseech thee, the voice of the Lord, which
I speak unto thee: so it shall be well unto thee,
and thy soul shall live.*   Jeremiah 38:20

"It shall be well unto thee, and thy soul shall live."
That should be motivation enough for any Christian to seek to understand the mysteries of hearing the voice of God. This promise is logical. If Christ is Head of the Church, and He is; if He is our Savior and Lord, and He is; if the Church is His Church, and it is; if the Word is His Word, and it is; if eternal life is His life, and it is; then it behooves every one of us to be in touch with Him on a regular basis. We need to hear His voice.

What will it do for you? The answers are endless:

I remember a woman who came into one of my meetings many years ago in West Point, Virginia. She said, "God has been speaking to me about visiting a friend of mine who is attending William and Mary University. The trouble is that I don't know exactly where she lives. What should I do?"

I said, "If God is telling you to go, you should go."

"But how will I find my friend?" she asked.

"I don't know," I told her, "But if God tells you to go there, He will have to help you with the details." And that is just what happened.

She prayed about what day to go and what time to leave. She prayed before leaving home for the twenty-five or thirty mile drive to the University. Arriving at the University, she found a parking place, then felt led to stand on a certain corner and wait. Within fifteen minutes, her friend passed by and she was able to fulfill her mission. And that's the way hearing the voice of God should work for every believer on every occasion.

He wants to help you with your day-to-day affairs of life. Before you make any business deal, get in touch with God and find out if that's what God wants you to do. He wants you to be successful and will help you — if you bother to ask for His help.

We had a friend in Maryland that was in the excavation business. Some years ago God spoke to him and told him He wanted to bless him. He loved the Lord, and was a generous giver to the church and to missions.

He was asked to make a bid on a sizable job. He took all the measurements, figured up his costs in labor and material, and prepared his estimate. At the last minute, he felt that since God was dealing with him about special blessing, he should put a higher than normal markup on the job. He really believed that doing that would not cause him to lose the job, but would result in blessing for the Kingdom.

When he was ready to make his final draft, God spoke to him and said, "Now double it." He found that hard to comprehend because he was sure that he had not only covered himself but that he would make a comfortable profit for himself and more to be used for the Lord's work. He even wondered if doubling the estimate might cause him to lose the job completely, and he was hoping that this would just be the first of many contracts with this particular company.

He was sure God was telling him to double the price, so he did; and the end result was that he got the contract, did the work to the company's satisfaction, and cleared a nice profit for himself and for the Lord's work. God knows just how to do it.

We can understand that case a little better because money is involved and because it has a practical application. But God is able to do the same for each of us in our particular areas of concern in life. Since He knows everything, He can help you with anything and with everything.

He is not only able to help you make money, He can help you save money by showing you how to make wise purchases. For instance, He can help you to find just the car you need at just the price you can afford.

Admiring the good deal I had gotten on a used car in Rocky Mount, North Carolina, a brother in our church once asked me, "Can I pray and ask God to give me a good automobile?"

I said, "Sure."

He said, "Can I pray that God would show me where to go and buy it?"

I said, "Of course you can."

He said, "Well, just how do I do that?"

I said, "Well, you may be riding down the road one day and pass some car lot and have a bad feeling about it. If that happens, you should go on searching until you come to a lot that gives you a sense of peace. You'll know, then, that God is leading you.

"They may show you many cars, trying to sell what they have in stock, but none of them may appeal to you. But when you see the car that God has for you, you will be drawn to it immediately."

"Do you really think it works that way?" he asked.

I said, "Just try it."

You would have to know the man to appreciate what happened. Not long afterward I saw him again and he was "as happy as a June bug," as we sometimes say in the South. He followed my suggestion and found exactly the car he wanted. The price was right, and the car proved to be reliable.

What It Will Do For Us

When I told him what to do, I was speaking by experience. God had done it for me already many times. Once I went into Richmond to look at some trucks that National Linen was selling. When I opened the door of one that looked like it would meet our needs, God told me to offer them half the asking price. After I had looked at it, I went into the shop and asked, "Where's the boss?"

The man said, "He's in the office. He's a hard boss."

I said, "So is mine."

"What do you want for that truck?" I asked, after I was seated in the boss's office.

When he told me how much he wanted, I said, "I'll give you half that much."

He fell over his desk like I had shot him, but when he raised up, he said, "I'll take it," and we bought the truck and got a lot of good use out of it.

Believe me, God is concerned about these things. He is concerned about every detail of your life. If you are willing to trust His judgment, He will help you with absolutely everything.

His Word declares:

No good thing will he withhold from them that walk uprightly.   Psalms 84:11

God wants to speak to every one of us and minister to the needs of our spirit, our mind, our bodies and our pocketbooks. His highest wish is for our personal prosperity. As He said:

> *Beloved, I wish above all things that thou mayest prosper and be in health, even as thy soul prospereth.* 3 John 1:2

Financial prosperity! Health! Spiritual prosperity! These are God's desires for His people, and they certainly represent what each of us would desire for ourselves. But we can never achieve these goals in life if we cannot learn to hear the voice of God. Prosperity comes through hearing and obeying His voice.

> *Keep therefore the words of this covenant, and do them, that ye may prosper in all that ye do.* Deuteronomy 29:9

How can you be faithful to God if you don't know what He expects of you? How can you obey Him if you don't know what that obedience requires?

Therefore, hearing the voice of God can turn your life around, giving you a purpose for living and lending you a grace and an air of certainty that will affect absolutely everything you do.

Learning to hear the voice of God will totally revolutionize your life and the lives of those around you.

When you know what God is saying, it brings

What It Will Do For Us

peace to your spirit. For many years I had been feeling that we should try to buy the properties adjoining our campground in Ashland, Virginia. The problem was that for eighteen years not a single property came up for sale. Then two houses came onto the market at about the same time. I was preparing for a trip to Australia, so I didn't have much time in which to make a proper decision about buying either or both of them.

When I went to look at one of the properties, I noticed that the yard didn't drain well. In fact, there was a foot of water left standing under the house. That didn't look good at all. I put a tentative deposit on the property, but it certainly wasn't too late to back out.

One morning, as I was praying, I asked God about that situation. "God," I said, "my time is running out. I must know quickly whether to buy that house or not." There was a Bible in the prayer room. I walked over to it and opened the pages. It opened to the story of Elisha coming back to the house of the Shunamite when her son had suddenly died. It read:

Then he returned, and walked in the house to and fro; and went up, and stretched himself upon him: and the child sneezed seven times, and the child opened his eyes.　　　2 Kings 4:35

That word gave me peace that I did not need to worry about taking immediate action on the house. If God had said I would walk back and forth in it, He knew that I had time still to make a more judicious decision.

Twice, while I was in Australia, Mother called me about the house. Other people were interested in it and the real estate agent said he needed our decision. We didn't want someone else to buy it, yet did we really want it? I was still troubled about not being able to keep the water out of the foundation and didn't know exactly what to do.

"Mother," I answered, "all I know is that God told me that when I return I'll walk 'to and fro' through that house. I guess we should go ahead and buy it." And we did, getting a good reduction because of the problems involved. I was grateful that I bought that house based on the word the Lord gave me that day in prayer.

Hearing the voice of God will save you from a world of problems. The treasurer of our church and camp had the tradition for many years of having all our camp staff to her house for a meal on Christmas Eve. She would prepared some hot apple cider and shoo-fly pies for all the Yankee folks, and, for us southern folks, some peach and apple pies. It was a lovely time of fellowship. Later, when the camp family got too large, we had to move that celebration to the main dining room of the camp. One Christmas

What It Will Do For Us

Eve, when we were still able to accept her invitation, I was approaching her house when God spoke to me and said, "Roll up the carpet in Sister Weidemann's living room." It was a lovely white one made in China.

When I got inside, I told her, "As I was coming across the yard, God told me that we should roll up your white carpet."

"Well, let's do that, then," she agreed.

I got another brother to help me, and we rolled up the carpet, carried it down the hallway, and placed it in one of the bedrooms.

The children were served first that night. The very first child came through the line, filled his plate with a special helping of banana cream pudding, walked from the dining room over to the living room and spilled his plate right in the middle of the floor — right where that lovely white Chinese carpet would have been — had we not heard the voice of God and moved it.

God is interested in your carpet. He is interested in every detail of your life and will protect your belongings if you can only hear His voice.

Sometimes we are dealing in matters of life and death, and we cannot make a mistake or do what we think. We must know what God is saying. In 1973, we were forced to postpone our scheduled tour of the Holy Land because of the Yom Kippur War. We waited one week, then, because the fighting was still going on, we postponed the trip a second week. On Saturday, God spoke to me and said, "The war will be over Monday morning." I called the district manager of SAS in Washington and told him, "We can reschedule that trip now because the war will be over on Monday. I would like to fly out on Tuesday."

He wasn't crazy about the idea of flying fifty-two people into the middle of a war zone and tried to talk me out of it. What would it hurt, he asked, to wait until all hostilities had ended before rescheduling? He went on for about thirty minutes, trying to convince me. But I could not be convinced. "God told me the war will be over on Monday morning," I insisted. "We can go."

He said, "I am forced to send you a telegram officially declaring that SAS will not be responsible for you or any of your passengers if you get yourself in trouble on this trip."

"That's fine," I said. "I will take full responsibility."

On Sunday morning, I declared on our live radio program that the war would be over the next day. And it happened just as God had shown me. As it turned out, it seems that Henry Kissinger had been in Moscow for talks, and when he got no help from the Russians, he headed for China, hoping to force the hand of the communist world to call off their Arab clients. Since the Russians could not permit it to look like China had been instrumental in ending the war, they were forced to end it themselves. The decision formally ending the war was announced before Kissinger landed in Beijing.

On Monday morning, when we awoke, newspaper headlines declared the end of the war, and the next day we flew into the Middle East in safety, just as God had shown us.

God is reliable. We can count on His word. He will never lead us astray. He will help us, even on a personal level. One day, my nephew David was going to take a group of people who had been attending the camp to the airport. It was a very hot summer day, and he thought it would be nice to take them in an air-conditioned car, so he sent another brother to the platform to ask if he could borrow my car. David has been like my own son, but for some reason I felt restrained when I prayed about the matter.

"Tell David he can't use my car," I told the brother.

David had been sitting in the back of the Tabernacle, and I noticed that when the brother conveyed to him this message, he was upset by it and sat there in silence for a few minutes, mulling over the situation. Then, not knowing what else to do, he got up and took the folks in one of the camp vans.

They hadn't gotten very far down the road when he came upon a terrible accident. A car traveling at a hundred miles an hour had missed the curve and run head on into a dump truck loaded with gravel. The two young boys in the car had been instantly killed. David was the first to arrive and was able to direct traffic on the scene until the police arrived. Then he went on to the airport.

Later, when he told me the story, I said, "David, you are alive because I obeyed God. If you had taken the car and gone, you would have been in front of that truck and might have been killed."

What can it do for us to hear the voice of God? Anything and everything. Since He is the Source of all wisdom, the Source of all financial supply, hearing what He is saying can make all the difference in your life.

This makes it imperative that we learn to recognize the ways in which God speaks to us.

PART II

HOW GOD
SPEAKS TO HIS PEOPLE

CHAPTER FIVE

THROUGH HIS WORD

*In the beginning was the Word, and the Word
was with God, and the Word was God. The same
was in the beginning with God. All things were
made by him; and without him was not any thing
made that was made. In him was life; and the life
was the light of men. And the light shineth in darkness; and the darkness comprehended it not.*

John 1:1-5

In some mysterious way, God has invested His
Word with Himself. Jesus, in whom *"all the fulness
of the Godhead"* dwelled, became *"the Word."* The
Bible, the Word of God, is much more than a holy
book. It is the expression of God to man. As such, it
becomes *"a lamp unto [our] feet"* and *"a light unto [our]
pathway,"* a road map for daily living.

Because of this unique aspect of the Word of God,
the preaching of the Word is very important. We
must never take it for granted and must never allow it to become commonplace. Every man or
woman who is called to preach should recognize

that just giving a sermon, any sermon, is not sufficient. God has something specific that He wants to
say to His people. We cannot simply repeat the same
things over and over. The people we are ministering to today are unique and have unique needs. If
God has called us to preach His Word, we have a
responsibility to seek His face until we know what
specific message to deliver each time we have the
opportunity to declare His Counsel.

If we are careful to do this, the preaching of the
Word of God will never grow stale, or tiring or bor-
ing, but will remain ever fresh, ever new, and ever
challenging to the people of God. This is His desire.

The anointed and timely preaching of the Word
of God can accomplish great things. Through one
message from the Word, God can feed everyone
present — from tiny children to the elderly and from
the newest believer to the most mature saint. And
that is nothing short of a miracle. When we are teaching, in a secular sense, the first thing we do is to
divide people into groups of similar age and experience. Then we can teach them on their own level.
But God knows how to minister to us all on our own
level at the same time — through the anointed
preaching of His Word. What a miracle!

It is not uncommon to hear people say as they go
out the front door of the church, "That was just for
me. I needed that." The strange thing is that the next
person in line will say the very same thing. It seems

that the message was for everyone, if everyone recognized it and accepted it.

God speaks through your pastor. The sermon that he preaches on Sunday morning is not just something that he thought up the day before. If he is truly a man of God, he seeks God, asking God exactly what he should speak, and the message he delivers from the Word of God is exactly what you and I need to hear. It may step all over our toes, and we may not like it; but if we need it, and God gives it, let's be happy about it and accept it.

My father believed in preaching things straight. Sometimes someone would stop him at the door and ask, "Preacher, were you aiming that sermon at me today?"

He would smile and ask, "Were you guilty?"

"No," they would assure him.

"Then I wasn't preaching at you," he would respond, and they were satisfied.

When God gives a message to His servants, however, the truth is that He is speaking to every one of us. His message is for every member of the Body and each of us should receive it personally.

The Word of God is the absolute authority for our lives and will never change. Jesus said:

Heaven and earth shall pass away, but my words
shall not pass away.   Matthew 24:35

Many who claim to want to know the will of God spend very little time in His Word. Learning the Word of God is important for two reasons: (1) God can speak to you directly through His Word, and (2) It is by the Word of God that we are to judge all other input that we receive from whatever other source. Nothing that God says to us, in any way, through another person or otherwise, can be contrary to His Word.

Paul taught us that even if some angel should come teaching something contrary to the Word of God, we must reject it. *"Let him be accursed,"* he wrote:

> *But though we, or an angel from heaven, preach any other gospel unto you than that which we have preached unto you, let him be accursed.*
>
> Galatians 1:8

This is serious business. The Word is pure and to be honored. If a voice speaks to you something contrary to the Word of God, you can know immediately that it wasn't the voice of God. A voice that speaks contrary to the Word of God has only one source, Satan, the deceiver, the angel of light. You may call it "flesh" or "self" or anything else, but the source is the same.

This general rule of ignoring anything that is not in keeping with the teachings of the Word of God can keep us out of a LOT of trouble. When we hear someone say that God has spoken to them, but what they express is contrary to the teachings of the Bible, we can know immediately that they didn't hear from God. No prophecy can be contrary to the Word of God, and if it does contradict the Word, you can safely ignore it, knowing that it cannot be from God. No dream or vision can contradict the Word of God. No preaching that contradicts the Word of God is inspired by Him. No counsel given to you by supposedly wise individuals can contradict the Word of God. NOTHING can contradict the Word. It is the final authority. Period!

This is why God has commanded each of us to study the Word. No single verse in the Bible expresses it better than Paul's teaching to Timothy:

> *Study to shew thyself approved unto God, a workman that needeth not to be ashamed, rightly dividing the word of truth.*   2 Timothy 2:15

Because the Word is unfailing and sure, you can act upon what you read. If you are not feeling well, and you read, *"I am the Lord that healeth thee,"* you can get up and start moving about and know that you will be able to fulfill your responsibilities. God cannot permit His Word to fail. Because He is unfailing, His Word is unfailing. It is *"yea"* and *"amen"*:

For all the promises of God in him are yea, and in him Amen, unto the glory of God by us.

2 Corinthians 1:20

If you have a need and you read in the Bible about Jehovah Jireh, the Lord that provides, you can stand on that promise and say to God, "You said You are our Provider. On the basis of that, I am taking action, stepping out by faith, expecting Your provision." That isn't presumptuous, and it doesn't anger God. The Bible is His Word, and He will always stand behind it. You can count on that fact.

If you are feeling sad or despondent or restless within your spirit, you may read about Him who is the Prince of Peace. In that moment, turn to Him for consolation and you will surely find it. He has said:

Peace I leave with you, my peace I give unto you: not as the world giveth, give I unto you. Let not your heart be troubled, neither let it be afraid.

John 14:27

The story is told of a Korean man who spent many years in solitary confinement for his faith. He had smuggled a copy of the Gospel of John inside, and, to maintain his sanity, he memorized all twenty-one chapters. Not long after he finished his memorization, the little book was discovered and destroyed; but it was too late. It was already hidden in his heart.

Through His Word

He could lie there at night and recite the Word of God verse by verse. Because of his faithfulness to the Word, the brainwashing techniques used against all the prisoners had no effect on him, and he came out of the prison well and strong. God's Word is powerful! Use it well.

In a time of serious decision making, you can always turn to the Word of God, without fear, knowing that it will lead you well. Don't just read the Bible for general teaching, expect God to give you specific and personal answers through His Word. Expect Him to give you just what you need at the moment.

From the time we were small children, our parents instilled in us the belief that the Word of God could speak to us, specifically and personally, at any time and about any circumstance. Some people find our habit of looking to the Word for specific instruction rather amusing. But we have found that if you believe for it, God does it. What else can we say?

My mother developed a habit very early in life of opening her Bible each evening expecting the Lord to give her some special direction from the Word. She would come home from church and hang her hat and coat in the hall closet. Then, even though she might have a house full of company, she would go into her bedroom, kneel down beside her bed, and talk to Jesus, expecting to receive from Him some specific word. Usually she got up with something specific from the Lord.

When my sister spent many months in Nepal for the Gospel's sake, one night the Lord gave my mother a Bible verse, three different times, that spoke of "the sleep of death." Sensing that Ruth was in danger, Mother was able to intercede before God for her.

No information was coming from Nepal, and we had no idea what might be happening, but later we learned that several attempts had been made on Ruth's life. First, someone set fire to her room, hoping that she would be burned alive. The fire went out when it reached her Bible on the table.

Next, her room was broken into and her fur stole and camera were stolen. She was not there at the time, so she was not harmed.

More seriously (and the thing that God has shown Mother through that word), someone had poisoned Ruth. She fell into a deep sleep that lasted three days and three nights. It must have been during this time that God alerted Mother and caused her to intercede on Ruth's behalf. When my sister woke up from that deep sleep, she was still groggy for another eighteen hours, but her life had been spared.

Another, rather humorous example of how God speaks, also involved Ruth. I was preparing to leave for Indiana to attend a conference. Ruth was also invited, but there were many things to be done and she wasn't sure she should go, and, since she was scurrying here and there, fulfilling a number of obligations, she really hadn't had time to seriously consider the matter.

Finally, I saw that time was running out, so I said to her. "Ruth, if you're going with me, you need to get ready. I have to leave very soon now."

She said, "Would you please get a scripture from the Lord and see if I'm supposed to go with you?"

I prayed and put my finger in the Bible. The verse that I read said:

And Ruth the Moabitess said unto Naomi, Let me now go to the field, and glean ears of corn after him in whose sight I shall find grace. And she said unto her, Go, my daughter.   Ruth 2:2

Since Indiana is corn country, we didn't think there was any doubt about God's will for Ruth at that moment. She got ready quickly and went with me, and we had a wonderful time of ministry in the Hoosier State.

I would have thought that the Ruth of the Bible went to the barley field or the wheat field, but, no. It was the corn field. God knows just how to speak to us and show us His will.

When I was in North Carolina one year praying about whether I should extend the time of my meetings, God gave me a word from the verse concerning the wounding of Mephibosheth because his nurse *"made haste to flee"*:

> *And Jonathan, Saul's son, had a son that was lame of his feet. He was five years old when the tidings came of Saul and Jonathan out of Jezreel, and his nurse took him up, and fled: and it came to pass, as she made haste to flee, that he fell, and became lame. And his name was Mephibosheth.*
>
> 2 Samuel 4:4

When I read that I knew that I should not be in a hurry to leave, so I extended my meetings one more week. At the end of that week, the Lord told me to extend another week. When the meeting finally closed, I felt at peace that I had done the will of God and many were blessed because of it.

In the early days of my ministry, I was preaching a revival in one of our branch churches. After the Sunday morning service several carloads of our people went with us to the radio station to make a broadcast. While we were on the air, the pastor of the church handed me a note that read: "It's up to you whether we go on another week."

I prayed, "God, help me to decide" and I opened my Bible. The verse my eyes fell on spoke of Paul returning to Jerusalem. When my turn came to speak, therefore, I knew what I should do and said, "This is the last night of the revival at the Calvary

Pentecostal Tabernacle here in Callao, Virginia. If you want to get in on this, don't miss tonight's service."

The people of the church were not very happy with that decision. Some of their relatives had promised to come the following week and they were sure that I had missed God's will for the meeting. About three that afternoon it began to snow and by seven we had six inches of snow on the ground. The roads became very dangerous to drive on and, later, were closed altogether. Then everyone knew that I had been right to close the meetings.

I wasn't always so sure of what God was telling me. Once I asked God if I should close a meeting and on both sides of the page I read, "Go home." I wanted confirmation, so I continued to pray and got the same answer. In fact God gave me the same answer nine different times. Now, some would say that was wonderful to get so many confirmations and have the assurance that you are doing the right thing, but it was not wonderful. If I had been spiritually mature, I would have acted on the first answer and required no more. My insistence on seeking God until He had to tell me the same thing over and over nine times was an indication of my immaturity at the time.

It is one thing to say, "God, I am like Solomon as he began his reign over the people. I don't know how to come in or to go out." But it is another thing entirely to require God to tell us something over and over before we are willing to believe Him and act on it. If we need nine confirmations we are either not hearing clearly or our flesh is unwilling to obey what God is saying.

The following morning, when I put my suitcase in the car and was preparing to leave, the lady of the house where I had been staying came running out to catch me before I got away. "You have a long-distance phone call," she said. It was my mother saying that a friend of the family, a sister in the Lord, had died in Richmond and that I needed to be at her funeral by eleven o'clock. I left immediately and got to Richmond twenty minutes before the funeral began. God had known all along what I needed to do, but I was just slow to hear His voice.

I told you about the case of the house I wasn't sure we should buy and the verse God gave me to show me that I would walk "to and fro" in it. Well, nearly every word to describe every situation is found in the Bible and God can use a specific portion that has just the words you need to hear to speak to you clearly and unmistakably.

One morning, another brother and I were on our way into Sydney, Australia on Quantas Airways, when they started serving breakfast. The other brother had already decided to fast, but I thought I would eat. When I saw what they were serving, I was more convinced than ever. They had two kinds of meat, eggs, fresh fruit and sweet rolls. Then, suddenly, I began to feel that I should fast too. After seeing the good food they were serving, I didn't like the idea of fasting. I said, "God, if You want me to fast, just give me a scripture that makes it clear to me." My Bible was laying on the seat beside me, and I opened it. It fell open to the verse:

> *Go, gather together all the Jews that are present in Shushan, and fast ye for me, and neither eat nor drink three days, night or day: I also and my maidens will fast likewise; and so will I go in unto the king, which is not according to the law: and if I perish, I perish.*   *Esther 4:16*

By the time the stewardess got to my seat with one of the hot trays in her hand and asked politely, "Would you like breakfast?" I had made my decision.

"Just bring me a cup of coffee," I replied.

She put back my tray with the two kinds of meat and the eggs, but she put in its place another tray with sweet rolls and fresh fruit. Just then my companion, who had been sitting in another part of the plane, came over with his tray. Since he was not eating, he was going to give me his portion too. Under the circumstances, it was very tempting to eat; but I knew God had spoken to me and I was determined to obey Him. As it turned out, we fasted the entire time we were in Australia, and we experienced great revival in every place.

There are so many things in God's wonderful book that He can use it to lead you — if you trust Him. Many years ago, as I was getting dressed for a service, the Lord spoke to me to receive an offering of $2,000 that night. It was long enough ago that it seemed like $20,000 to me at the time. What God was saying was so astounding that I felt I needed some confirmation. I opened the Bible and my eyes fell on the verse:

> *Now therefore, I pray thee, give pledges to my lord the king of Assyria, and I will deliver thee two thousand horses, if thou be able on thy part to set riders upon them.* 2 Kings 18:23

When it came time for the offering, I got up and told the people what God had shown me, and the $2,000 came in quicker than if I had tried to get $200. God knows just how to do it.

Some years ago, I was involved in a court case in Covington, Virginia. I was new to this and was a little troubled in my spirit, not knowing what to expect. As I prayed that morning, God gave me a Scripture:

> *Heal me, O Lord, and I shall be healed; save me, and I shall be saved: for thou art my praise. Be-*

hold, they say unto me, Where is the word of the Lord? let it come now. As for me, I have not hastened from being a pastor to follow thee: neither have I desired the woeful day; thou knowest: that which came out of my lips was right before thee. Be not a terror unto me: thou art my hope in the day of evil. Let them be confounded that persecute me, but let not me be confounded: let them be dismayed, but let not me be dismayed: bring upon them the day of evil, and destroy them with double destruction. Jeremiah 17:14-18

I went into court that day with a wonderful assurance that God was on my side and would fight for me. The lawyer on the other side of the table seemed to have a smirk on his face, as if he were about to win an easy case, but during the proceedings he became so confused that we walked out with an easy victory.

I could go on, giving hundreds of examples, because this works. God speaks through His Word, in a general sense and in a specific and personal sense.

Some people are not happy with the scripture they get, so they keep picking scriptures until they get the one they want. Don't be guilty of making a mockery of this method of hearing from God. Believe for it and start hearing the voice of God through His Word.

CHAPTER SIX

THROUGH DREAMS AND VISIONS

And it shall come to pass afterward, that I will pour out my spirit upon all flesh; and your sons and your daughters shall prophesy, your old men shall dream dreams, your young men shall see visions:　　　　　　　　　　Joel 2:28

Some might think, based on this promise, that only *"old men"* have spiritual dreams, but that is certainly not true. Solomon was young when he had a dream, a dream that was to change his life forever:

In Gibeon the Lord appeared to Solomon in a dream by night: and God said, Ask what I shall give thee. ... And God said unto him, Because thou hast asked this thing, and hast not asked for thyself long life; neither hast asked riches for thyself, nor hast asked the life of thine enemies; but hast asked for thyself understanding to discern judgment; Behold, I have done according to thy words: lo, I have given thee a wise and an understanding heart; so that there was none like thee before thee, neither after thee shall any arise like unto thee. And I have also given thee that which thou hast not asked, both riches, and honour: so that there shall not be any among the kings like unto thee all thy days. And if thou wilt walk in my ways, to keep my statutes and my commandments, as thy father David did walk, then I will lengthen thy days. And Solomon awoke; and, behold, it was a dream.   1 Kings 3:5, 11-15

The results of this dream and its fulfillment in the life of Solomon are legendary. He could never be the same again.

Spiritual dreams and visions were common among God's people from earliest times. The ancient patriarchs, Abraham, Isaac, Jacob and Joseph, had such dreams. Joseph got in trouble because he spoke too readily of his dreams to his brothers, who did not share his spirituality.

Job, one of the oldest men of Bible times, spoke of dreams and visions:

In a dream, in a vision of the night, when deep sleep falleth upon men, in slumberings upon the bed;   Job 33:15

Most all of the prophets of God experienced dreams and visions. Daniel was one of those:

In the first year of Belshazzar king of Babylon

Through Dreams and Visions

Daniel had a dream and visions of his head upon
his bed: then he wrote the dream, and told the sum
of the matters. Daniel 7:1

Jeremiah gave instructions for prophets to share
their dreams with others around them:

The prophet that hath a dream, let him tell a dream;
and he that hath my word, let him speak my word
faithfully ... saith the Lord. Jeremiah 23:28

In the New Testament, God spoke to Joseph
through a dream and told him not to worry about
Mary being pregnant out of wedlock, because it was
for a divine purpose:

But while he thought on these things, behold, the
angel of the Lord appeared unto him in a dream,
saying, Joseph, thou son of David, fear not to take
unto thee Mary thy wife: for that which is con-
ceived in her is of the Holy Ghost.
Matthew 1:20

After the birth of the Child, God spoke to Joseph
again in a dream, showing him to leave that place
quickly because there were some men who wanted
to kill the Child:

And when they were departed, behold, the angel

*of the Lord appeareth to Joseph in a dream, say-
ing, Arise, and take the young child and his
mother, and flee into Egypt, and be thou there
until I bring thee word: for Herod will seek the
young child to destroy him.* Matthew 2:13

Later, when Joseph and Mary were living in
Egypt, God spoke to him in another dream and told
him that it now was safe to return to *"the land of Israel"*:

*But when Herod was dead, behold, an angel of
the Lord appeareth in a dream to Joseph in Egypt,
Saying, Arise, and take the young child and his
mother, and go into the land of Israel: for they are
dead which sought the young child's life. And he
arose, and took the young child and his mother,
and came into the land of Israel.*

Matthew 2:19-21

Even unbelievers sometimes received dreams
from God, and the servants of the Lord were expected to be able to interpret these dreams. Joseph
interpreted the dreams of his fellow prisoners and,
later, of the Pharaoh and revealed the seven years
of fatness and the seven years of leanness that were
to come upon Egypt and the surrounding areas.
Daniel interpreted the dreams of Nebuchadnezzar,
King of Babylon.

Through Dreams and Visions

The most important thing about dreams is not to dismiss them outrightly. We all know that not all dreams are from God, that some dreams are caused by what you eat or by how tired you are when you go to bed or by what you might have on your mind at the moment. But to dismiss every dream as being the result of eating too much cabbage is very dangerous. And that is exactly what many Christians do.

Solomon received the fulfillment of his dream because he believed his dream and worked toward it. Joseph's brothers did indeed bow down to him, although he was younger than most of them, because he believed his dreams and was faithful to God until they came to pass.

If you immediately dismiss every dream with some cute reasoning ("too much Coca-cola" is a favorite of many), you are not giving God a chance to speak to you in this way and may be missing something important He wants to show you at the time.

When I was a young boy, eleven or twelve years old, I was chosen to be a member of the safety patrol squad at school. One night I had a dream that I had been voted in as captain of the squad. The dream was so real that I told my mother about it before I left for school the next morning. When I came home for lunch I couldn't wait to tell her that my dream had come true. That day, in a special meeting of all the members of the safety patrol, I was elected captain.

Most of us understand what dreams are like because they are common to everyone. Children begin to dream very early and often talk in their sleep because their dreams seem real. They may or may not remember the dream later. A vision is just like a dream, but it happens while you are awake. Job called a dream *"a vision of the night."* In the same way, we could call a vision a dream when you are awake. In a vision, your eyes may be closed or they may be open. It really doesn't matter.

I even believe that what we call "daydreams" are often visions from God. So we should not dismiss our daydreams out of hand. Some understand what we mean by "visions" better if we refer to them as simply a "picture."

Dreams and visions are ways that God has of speaking to the subconscious mind, the spirit of man. Your spirit never rests. It is always awake and able to receive instruction. Job captured the essence of this truth, when he said:

> *For God speaketh once, yea twice, yet man perceiveth it not. In a dream, in a vision of the night, when deep sleep falleth upon men, in slumberings upon the bed; Then he openeth the ears of men, and sealeth their instruction.*
>
> Job 33:14-16

Your body sleeps but your spirit is awake all night long and if you'll be open to the spirit of God, the

Lord will come and speak to you in dreams. He can speak to you, open your ears, and seal your instruction — while you are sleeping. What a wonderful blessing! This makes it all the more terrible when people dismiss their dreams without even giving them a second thought. As Job said, *"Man perceiveth it not."* He also said concerning dreams:

> *He shall fly away as a dream, and shall not be found: yea, he shall be chased away as a vision of the night.* Job 20:8

Dreams easily *"fly away"* or are *"chased away"* by those who dismiss them as nonsense. Don't be guilty of taking lightly a means by which God wants to share with you the treasures of His Kingdom. If you will contend for everything God shows you in dreams and visions, He will surely bring it to pass.

Some dreams are warnings and will not necessarily come to pass if we take heed to God's warnings and do what He shows us.

I have had Christians tell me that they had dreams in which they were smoking again or drinking again or doing something else they had been delivered from long ago. They were shocked by the dream and asked me to pray for them. They certainly didn't want to backslide and return to their former life. If you have such a dream, it could be that God is showing you that there is something in your life that is not pleasing to Him. The smoking or drinking is something you can easily recognize, but the real problem may be something totally unrelated. Seeing yourself doing something so obviously unclean and displeasing to God can shake you into recognizing how terrible it is to backslide and can keep you from sin and shipwreck.

Clearly, not all dreams are from God, and even godly dreams require interpretation. They are often given to you in allegory or in symbolism. You can't take every dream literally and you can't place the interpretation that best suits your fancy on it either. God knows what He means, and we want to know what He means, not what we might think He means. God has placed people in the Body with special gifts in this area:

And Daniel had understanding in all visions and dreams. Daniel 1:17

Forasmuch as an excellent spirit, and knowledge, and understanding, interpreting of dreams, and shewing of hard sentences, and dissolving of doubts, were found in the same Daniel, whom the king named Belteshazzar: now let Daniel be called, and he will shew the interpretation.

Daniel 5:12

In the third year of Cyrus king of Persia a thing was revealed unto Daniel, whose name was called

Through Dreams and Visions

Belteshazzar; and the thing was true, but the time
appointed was long: and he understood the thing,
and had understanding of the vision.

Daniel 10:1

As spiritual as we might be, we need to submit
our dreams and visions to those who are over us in
the Lord, our pastors, our spiritual parents, and we
need to listen carefully to their wise counsel. They
often know more of the overall picture when we
might see only a small portion. It is always good to
have balance. Never go off on some tangent based
on a dream or vision you have received.

On the other hand, never submit your dreams to
those who are less spiritual than you for interpretation. You may get any old thing as an interpretation.
God's will is too important to be playing around
with it like small children.

If God gives you a dream, ask Him to show you
the meaning, but if you need help, don't hesitate to
call on those who are gifted in this area.

Another error that is often made by immature believers is in the timing of the dream. This was
Joseph's problem. The dreams were real, but he revealed them prematurely, before anyone could
understand what they meant. If a dream is real and
God inspired, and you still can't get understanding
of it, it may well be for a future time. Put it in the
back of your mind or, as the Bible says, "hide it in

your heart," and wait for a future time. If God has shown you something now that is for a future time, He is allowing you time to prepare. Take advantage of the opportunity. Don't just dismiss the dream or vision because you don't understand it fully or it seems presently impossible.

Dreams and visions can be a great blessing to your life — if you believe them and act upon them. My father always said that Mother was the Joseph[ine] in our family, since she was the one to have dreams and to receive the interpretation of dreams. Although she had more dreams than him, however, my father also occasionally had dreams that he felt were from God. The key for him was that he forgot most dreams and could not bring them to mind again. If he could remember a dream, he was certain that it was from the Lord, and he was not afraid to act on it.

Dreams and visions can also become a ministry to other people. As God show you things about other people, you might prophesy what you are seeing. If the person is not present, you may pray about a time when you can share your dream with them.

Sometimes, when we have a dream, we don't understand anything about it, but are led to tell someone else. When we tell them, they understand it perfectly.

Just as God gives you personal dreams that are not to be shared until a future time, He may show you things about someone else that you cannot tell them. In fact, your participation in the dream may be just to pray or just to aid the person in some way to achieve the goal God has set before them. So don't tell everything.

And sometimes there is nothing you can do but pray. When I was weak and dying from Typhoid Fever overseas and had no way to contact my father, for he was traveling in Israel at the time, a lady in our church had a dream about it. She told the whole church, and together they were able to intercede on our behalf.

God had shown my mother, as well, and I had a dream that she and Ruth were coming to help us. I told my companion, who was also seriously ill, not to worry because someone was coming to help us. It was the Lord who was coming to our rescue. Our lives were spared. Praise God for His faithfulness!

When you have had a dream about someone else, and they need to do something to bring it to pass, you can't force them to obey, even though you would like to sometimes. I once had a dream about a certain preacher going with me on a trip around the world. I waited a few days, then I called him and told him what I had seen.

"Brother Heflin," he said, "you know I would love to go with you, but I can't."

I said, "Will you pray about it and ask God?"

He promised he would, but after a week or so he

called and told someone in the tour office to tell me that he couldn't go.

A couple more weeks went by, and I saw his phone number laying on my desk one day and called him again.

"Didn't you get my message?" he said. "I don't see how I can go."

"All I can think about," I told him, "is the dream I had. I'm sure it was from God, and I don't want to go without you."

He said, "I'll pray about it."

Within an hour's time, he had called back to say that his passport and check were in the mail and that he would be joining us after all."

He was greatly blessed on the trip and only regretted not praying seriously about it a lot sooner.

God wants to speak to us even while we're sleeping — if we will let Him do it. When we don't take dreams seriously, or we allow others to discourage us from putting any faith in a dream, God has no choice but to stop speaking to us in this way. Don't let that happen. Start hearing the voice of God through dreams and visions.

CHAPTER SEVEN

THROUGH PROPHECY

This charge I commit unto thee, son Timothy, according to the prophecies which went before on thee, that thou by them mightest war a good warfare; 1 Timothy 1:18

God speaks to us in prophecy, and we must contend for everything He has said through this marvelous gift. I have said much on this subject in my book, *The Power of Prophecy*, so I won't repeat all of those teachings here. There are, however, several things that need to be said here.

When God has spoken to us, it gives us a tool to use against the Enemy of our souls. We can tell him, "Stand back, Satan, God said ..." And he must stand back.

I believe that a portion of every prophetic word given in a particular service is for everyone present. Sometimes every word is for everyone present, but usually only a portion is for everyone; and the rest may be for individuals present. I have learned to discern when prophecy, even if it is spoken over another individual, is for me, and I reach out to receive it.

Prophecy is of God. I am so convinced to that truth that I would risk my entire future on it. When God speaks to me, I hold that word tight to my bosom and write it indelibly on my heart. Then I begin to see what I can do to fulfill the requirements God has put forth in the prophecy. There are always some conditions that I must meet. And when I have done my part, God never fails to do His.

When God has spoken to you and told you that He will do something in your life, it makes no difference what the circumstances might be or what the Enemy may try to do to stop God's plan for you. It will come to pass — as you believe it and act on it.

The spoken word, a word given in prophecy over you, is just as sure as the written Word. If you refuse, however, to honor it, to cherish it, to hold it to your bosom and not let one word fall to the ground, God is not obligated to fulfill it. If you receive it and act on it, God is obligated to fulfill it, just as much as He is obligated to fulfill the written Word.

Through the years, God has blessed us as a church and as a family because of the prophetic gift of my Mother, a gift that my sister and I were challenged to develop and which has enhanced our ministry everywhere we go.

Too many people take prophecy lightly, and when they do, their prophetic promises never come to pass. Never blame God for these failures. He is faithful — when we do our part.

God may allow you to pass through many tests and trials before your promise is fulfilled. It happened to Job, yet in all his trials, Job never stopped trusting God and God's will for his life. He said:

Though he slay me, yet will I trust in him:
Job 13:15

When a doctor tells you to take a pill and, over time, you will start feeling better, if you trust him, you will take the pill and expect to feel better. With God, we don't seem to have even that much patience. If He doesn't do immediately what we think He ought to do, we get discouraged and want to find another way. But God has the right to test us.

Trials need not be troublesome to us. Abraham's faith was sorely tried, yet the Scriptures declare:

He staggered not at the promise of God through unbelief; but was strong in faith, giving glory to God; And being fully persuaded that, what he had promised, he was able also to perform. And therefore it was imputed to him for righteousness.
Romans 4:20-22

Stand on the promise God has given you. Know that it is *"sure"*:

Hear the Voice of God

We have also a more sure word of prophecy.
2 Peter 1:19

Conditions in the earth may well get more difficult, as greater darkness come upon the earth than
ever before. But we have nothing to fear. The Word
declares:

> *For, behold, the darkness shall cover the earth, and
> gross darkness the people: but the Lord shall arise
> upon thee, and his glory shall be seen upon thee.*
> Isaiah 60:2

The message you receive through prophecy also
has a correct timing to it. Some who hear the voice
of God through prophecy want to jump up and do
immediately what they are hearing. But just as God
gives us work to do, He tells us when and how and
with whom, and these details are just as important
as the task at hand.

Also, the stops of God are just as important as the
go's of God. Many become frustrated because they
get the initial revelation but do not wait to break
through into the details of how to fulfill it and when,
etc.

Some people seem to be using prophecy like some
sort of narcotic. Every time I see them they say the
same thing: "Brother Heflin, I need a word from
God." I am glad to help these people, glad to be used

of the Lord to minister to them, but I consider their dependence on others to know the will of God very dangerous, and I wouldn't want to be in their shoes.

There is nothing wrong with prophecy and nothing wrong with personal prophecy, but if you are one of those who are always looking for somebody to give them a word, you might get a word at some point that is not convenient. Jesus warned:

> *Not every one that saith unto me, Lord, Lord, shall enter into the kingdom of heaven; but he that doeth the will of my Father which is in heaven.*
> Matthew 7:21

There are people who don't fear God and who have their own agenda in life. Putting yourself into their hands is very dangerous and foolish. God said of some Old Testament pretenders:

> *I have not sent these prophets, yet they ran: I have not spoken to them, yet they prophesied.*
> Jeremiah 23:21

Be careful whose hand is laid on your head, and if you are careful, you will consistency hear from God, and your life will not be spiritually bankrupt and shipwrecked. Be one of His sheep who know His voice and will not listen to another.

You don't need a prophetic word every time you

turn around. This is not the way God wants to control and govern your life. He wants you to walk and talk with Him on a personal basis so that a maturity can come to your soul. As we will see in another section, you can never be a prophet or a prophetess yourself unless you can hear the voice of God. There are many other ministries that await you but which you can never perform if you can't hear the voice of God for yourself.

I get a little nervous with the proliferation of prophets and prophetic conferences in the world today, especially when I see the quality of the people who are attending them. I get a little nervous when someone hands me their calling card and it declares them to be a prophet. I have found that the fruit speaks for itself. When men and women know God and hear His voice, it is easy to see. They don't have to declare it. The Holy Ghost knows how to hoist the red flags in our spirit when we face insincere or hypocritical people.

But don't throw the baby out with the bath water. Just because there are insincere people in the world doesn't mean that you should avoid prophecy or stop prophesying. NEVER! Insist on hearing the voice of God through prophecy.

CHAPTER EIGHT

THROUGH AN AUDIBLE VOICE

*I was in the Spirit on the Lord's day, and heard
behind me a great voice, as of a trumpet, ... And I
turned to see the voice that spake with me.*
                                        Revelation 1:10 and 12

John heard the audible voice of God over and over
again as he was receiving his Revelation, during his
time on the Isle of Patmos. Although hearing the
voice of God audibly has become a rather rare oc-
currence among believers today, it should not be so.
It was in an audible voice that God spoke with Adam
and Eve in the beginning, and He has been doing it
ever since.

Moses heard the audible voice of God at the burn-
ing bush:

> *When Moses saw it, he wondered at the sight: and
> as he drew near to behold it, THE VOICE OF
> THE LORD came unto him,*   Acts 7:31

Samuel heard the voice of God as a small boy, and

it was so real that he thought it was Eli, the priest, calling him. Eli had grown cold in his own experience, for when Samuel came to him and asked him if he had called, he just answered, "Son, I didn't call you. Go back to bed."

When Samuel obeyed and went back to bed, it happened again. It was only after Samuel had heard the audible voice of God several times that Eli finally realized that it was the Lord. Then he advised Samuel to reply the next time, "Speak, Lord, for Your servant heareth."

Before long, it happened again, and Samuel did as he was instructed. God told Samuel that night that He was going to remove Eli from his office. That was a heavy burden for a small child to bear, yet Samuel showed wisdom in telling Eli the parts of his revelation that wouldn't be offensive to him and in guarding the rest in his spirit for a future time. It was because of this ability to hear the voice of God and use wisdom concerning the revelation that Samuel became one of the greatest prophets in the history of Israel. The Scriptures say of him:

And Samuel grew, and the Lord was with him, and did let none of his words fall to the ground. And all Israel from Dan even to Beersheba knew that Samuel was established to be a prophet of the Lord. And the Lord appeared again in Shiloh: for the Lord revealed himself to Samuel in Shiloh by

*the word of the Lord. And the word of Samuel
came to all Israel.* 1 Samuel 3:19-4:1

Other Old Testament prophets also heard the audible voice of God:

*Also I heard THE VOICE OF THE LORD, saying, Whom shall I send, and who will go for us?
Then said I, Here am I; send me.* Isaiah 6:8

During the time that Jesus was on the Earth, the Father's voice was heard audibly several times by those standing near the Master:

*And lo a voice from heaven, saying, This is my
beloved Son, in whom I am well pleased.*
Matthew 3:17

*While he yet spake, behold, a bright cloud over-shadowed them: and behold a voice out of the
cloud, which said, This is my beloved Son, in
whom I am well pleased; hear ye him.*
Matthew 17:5

*Then came there a voice from heaven, saying, I
have both glorified it [God's name], and will glo-rify it again. The people therefore, that stood by,
and heard it, said that it thundered: others said,
An angel spake to him. Jesus answered and said,*

Hear the Voice of God

*This voice came not because of me, but for your
sakes.*   John 12:28-30

Peter was one of those who heard the audible
voice of the Father and later wrote about it:

*For he received from God the Father honour and
glory, when there came such a voice to him from
the excellent glory, This is my beloved Son, in
whom I am well pleased. And this voice which
came from heaven we heard, when we were with
him in the holy mount.*   2 Peter 1:17-18

Saul heard the audible voice of God on the Road
to Damascus, an experience which led to his con-
version:

*And he fell to the earth, and heard a voice saying
unto him, Saul, Saul, why persecutest thou me?
And he said, Who art thou, Lord? And the Lord
said, I am Jesus whom thou persecutest: it is hard
for thee to kick against the pricks. And he trem-
bling and astonished said, Lord, what wilt thou
have me to do? And the Lord said unto him, Arise,
and go into the city, and it shall be told thee what
thou must do. And the men which journeyed with
him stood speechless, hearing a voice, but seeing
no man.*   Acts 9:4-7

Through An Audible Voice

Peter heard the audible voice of the Lord when he was praying on the housetop in Joppa:

And there came a voice to him, Rise, Peter; kill, and eat.   Acts 10:13

And the voice spake unto him again the second time, What God hath cleansed, that call not thou common.   Acts 10:15

Both of these men remembered the details of this experience clearly and often repeated them when sharing their stories. Paul said that those who were with him at the time saw a light and were afraid, but only he had heard the voice.

So, hearing the audible voice of God is a legitimate and desired experience that should be for us today, as well.

When God does speak in an audible voice, most of us react in the very same way those biblical personalities reacted. We look around to see who has spoken, and when we find no one, we wonder what exactly is happening.

At one period in my life, I heard someone at my front door calling my name and knocking. I shouted, "Wait a minute. I'll be right there." I got up, put my clothes on, and went to the door. But when I got there, no one was there. This happened several times. I thought maybe the person who was knocking got tired of waiting and was going away, so I shouted into the night, "Who's there?" But there was no response. I was never able to explain these experiences, but I got serious in prayer with God, sensing that He wanted to show me something.

Eli had the secret. If you hear a voice and you don't know whose voice it is, say "Yes, God," and make yourself available to Him. Who knows what the result might be?

When I think on this subject, our dear friend, Richard Lessing, from Fort Wayne, Indiana, always comes to mind. For many years he was a design engineer for International Harvester. (The company was later sold to a Japanese firm, and International Trucks became Navistar.) The company had laid off many workers, and Richard had been laid off several times; but, for some reason, he had been called back. God wasn't finished with him.

Sally, Richard's wife, had a great desire to go to the Holy Land one year, but Richard didn't want to go. She knew just what to do, and started praying on him. One day Richard came home from work, got on his tractor, and was riding down through the soybean patch when he heard a voice calling his name. He stopped, got off the tractor, and looked around to see who was calling him; but he didn't see anyone. The more he thought about the experience the more sure he became that God was trying to tell him something. The next day he was very anxious to get through his work and get home so that he could get on his tractor and ride out into the field again, hoping to find out what God was trying to tell him.

When he heard the same voice saying, "Jerusalem," he asked, "Lord, how can I afford a trip to Jerusalem?" The Lord's answer was, "I will multiply the soy beans so much that when you sell them you will have enough for both yourself and your wife to go." And that is exactly how it happened.

After that, the Lessings took other trips for the Lord. On one such trip, they and their son accompanied us to Russia. We had been commissioned of the Lord to do something special for the Jewish people in Russia, and it required delivering something to an apartment on Gorky Street in Moscow. Because of the danger involved, I wanted to take some strong man with me, and Richard was a strong man; but I chose him more so because I knew he could hear the voice of God. Russia is a very different place today and we thank God for the changes, but in those days if you walked down the streets of Moscow, you sensed that you needed someone who was sensitive to the Spirit's leading.

When we were arriving in Moscow from Leningrad (now returned to its former name, St. Petersburg), we had no idea just where we would be staying. Those things were under the control of the state-owned Inturist. As it happened, we stayed at the

Inturist Hotel on Gorky Street. On our way to the hotel, we were searching furtively for the house numbers, trying to locate the place we had to visit. Amazingly, it was only two blocks from our hotel.

While the others got settled into the hotel, I took Richard and started off to find our secret destination. The apartment was located on the 8th floor, and we supposed we would have to walk up the long, dark stairway. As we approached the entryway, however, suddenly a dark figure rose up out of the corner of the stairwell. It was very dark in there, and whoever it was scared the living daylights out of me. My heart jumped into my throat. As it turned out, it was a very little Russian man, the caretaker of the building, trying to indicate to us that there was an elevator. In the dimly lit entryway, we had missed it. Gratefully, we took it and went upstairs.

The man we were visiting was Vladimir Schlepik, a Russian dissident. He soon became one of the primary movers of the Soviet Protest Movement, was sentenced to five years in Siberia and later escaped to the West when his life was in serious danger.

"Who are you?" he asked us that night.

"I am a Pentecostal preacher from America," I told him and gave him the package that we had been asked to deliver.

He said, "I know many Pentecostal people here. There are many of them, and they are persecuted even more than our people. Often their children are taken from them because they refuse to forsake their religious views and are, thus, considered by the state to be unfit parents. When they are caught by the KGB in the bus stations or train stations or airports, trying to travel, their tickets are taken from them, torn up and thrown in the street.

I took off the Star of David tie tack that I was wearing and gave it to him. He reached out to grab it like a drowning man. That day he held a press conference on behalf of another of the dissidents, Anatoly Sharansky, who also was able to escape to the West later. I was so glad that I had heard the voice of the Lord to go to his aid and that I had a friend like Richard Lessing to help me.

The experience in the cornfield opened Richard to hearing God in many other ways and in the manifestation of the presence of angels with him. After that, he made many more exciting trips with us.

The audible voice of the Lord may call your name, and you may hear it behind you, at your side, or over your head.

Just as He did to Saul of Tarsus, the fearsome persecutor of the Church, sometimes God speaks in this way to sinners, just to shake them up a little. One man that we and our people were praying for told us that one day when he was in a bar drinking, he felt a tap on his shoulder. He looked around to see who had done it, and there was no one there. Troubled, he moved to the other side of the bar and got himself another beer. Then it happened again. This time, when he looked around, however, he heard a voice saying, "Go to church." He got out of that place quickly.

The next morning he knocked early on the door of his estranged wife and said to his daughter, "Get dressed, we're all going to church."

"Dad, are you drunk?" one of the kids asked. But he wasn't, and they all went to church. It wasn't long before the man was such a shining example of new life in Christ that he was asked to share in a Sunday School class.

Some would say that God doesn't go into bars, but I know differently. I remember one New Year's Eve, a few months before I got saved. I was in a bar, ready to have a good time. There was a fifth of whiskey on the table in front of me, but the more I drank the more sober I seemed to get, and the more miserable I felt in that place. I was six hundred miles from home, and I was twenty-nine years old and a successful salesman, but I could still hear my mother's voice saying, "Be a good boy, son. Jesus might come tonight."

It may not have come in an audible voice, but it was that constant and loving voice of God that eventually led me back to His paths.

Through An Audible Voice

Although God is able to speak audibly to us and wants to do it, many have never heard His voice in this way. I believe that if we can eliminate some of the things that hinder us more of us will be able in the near future to walk and talk with God in this very intimate way. Let us believe more for hearing the voice of God audibly.

CHAPTER NINE

THROUGH A STILL, SMALL VOICE

And he said, Go forth, and stand upon the mount before the Lord. And, behold, the Lord passed by, and a great and strong wind rent the mountains, and brake in pieces the rocks before the Lord; but the Lord was not in the wind: and after the wind an earthquake; but the Lord was not in the earthquake: And after the earthquake a fire; but the Lord was not in the fire: and after the fire a still small voice.   1 Kings 19:11-12

The prophet Elijah had a strange experience. God visited him in a very special way. But God wasn't in the wind or the earthquake or the fire, as we might have expected, but He was in the *"still small voice."* This still, small voice is the most common of all the ways that God speaks. I believe that is because God is a Spirit and He delights in bypassing the outward trappings and speaking directly to our spirits, as only He can.

The still, small voice is not audible at all. There is no sound. It comes from within. It almost seems, at times, more like a knowing than a voice. Suddenly you know something, something that you didn't know a minute ago, and it seems as though you have always known it. In reality, you have just learned it from the Lord through His still, small voice. This may be the reason that many confuse the voice of God with self or with other spiritual influences, but there is no comparison. God has the best communication system going. It beats anything on the market. It is direct — spirit to spirit.

Some people think that when God speaks to them they have to see flashing lights and hear sirens. When it happens, they miss it because it doesn't seem like anything earth-shattering. No whistles or bells go off. No lights flash. No sirens sound.

Many people have heard the voice of the Lord, I am sure, and never realized what they were hearing. They say things like, "Something told me to pick up the phone and call that person. I can't explain it. I wasn't aware of any existing problem. But when I called, the person said, 'I'm so happy that you called. I've been sick, and I needed someone to pray with me.' When I prayed, the person was healed."

That "something" that told you to make the call was the voice of the Lord. The devil doesn't tell you to call desperate people just when they need your help. The flesh doesn't lead you to pray for the sick and get them healed.

It's time for us to stop calling God "something.

He must get tired of that. He is not "something." He is not "some urge." He is not "some strange feeling" or "some sudden impulse." He is the God of the Universe.

Another reason that God speaks in the still, small voice is that He wants us to be so sensitive to His voice, so attuned to His touch, that we can detect even His most tender whispers. This also denotes the intimate nature of our relationship with Him. We no longer need Him to shout. Just a whisper will do.

The Scriptures speak of the marvel of a great ship being turned at sea by such a small rudder. This is what God wants for us, to turn us about with His gentle touch.

One evening, during camptime, a small child, a little girl, came up behind me and tapped me on the shoulder. Her touch was so light that I wasn't sure I was even feeling it. It was almost imperceptible. But I did feel it and I turned to see what she wanted. When it happened, I realized that this is what God wants of us, to be so sensitive to Him that we feel and understand His lightest touch. He wants to treat us with the utmost tenderness and receive our loving response.

It might be more correct to say of this intimate form of communication that God has suddenly dropped something into your spirit.

Compare this loving, intimate, communication

with God to the way many Christians are accustomed to discerning the will of God. A woman from another country came to attend our camp, but she got sick and was confined to her bed. After she missed several days of services, I went to pray for her. She said, "It's okay, Brother Heflin. Every time God wants to speak to me, He has to put me flat on my back."

I said, "If I were you, I wouldn't be so rebellious." I would hate for God to have to make me sick and not able to move every time He wanted to tell me something. What a terrible way to live!

God doesn't want to have to place you in some difficulty every time He wants to show you something. He doesn't want you to have an accident and be hospitalized just so that He can talk to you. Everyone who has this experience says, "That was so important. I needed to be in that bed, beside that person who needed the Lord." But God has better ways to evangelize the lost. If you are well, you can visit and witness to dozens of patients every day. Let God speak to you daily and you won't have to end up in a hospital bed.

When I was a very young Christian, God began to speak to me intimately. At first I didn't know to say it was God. I just said, "I feel," but I wasn't sure why I felt the way I did, and there was always a very wonderful result when I got those "feelings." Once I remember saying to my sister that I felt we should go to the John Marshall Hotel in Richmond to see if they had anything they wanted to give the camp. They had already blessed us with some furniture just a few months before, but somehow I felt there was more. Since it was just two weeks before Christmas, she imagined they might be too busy to attend to us. Since I "felt" strongly about it, however, she agreed to accompany me.

When we arrived at the office, the man in charge said to us, "I'm so glad to see you folks. We're giving up four floors of our warehouse, and we must have everything out of there by the 27th of December. Go over there and take a look to see if there is anything you can use. You can have anything and everything you find there." We had just finished building our first permanent building on the campground and had no furnishings for it. What a blessing that was for us!

We had no way to haul the things we found in the huge warehouse, so we rented a truck and packed it with chairs, sofas and beds. We took home four hundred bed ends made by Biggs (the finest antique reproduction people in the state of Virginia), twenty thousand bars of soap, sixteen hundred pieces of heavy-duty Syracuse restaurant china and many other useful things.

With those kinds of miracles happening, it didn't take me long to stop saying, "I feel," and to recognize that it was God who was putting His thoughts into my spirit. Now, when God says 'Go," I jump, because I know the greatness of what He can do when we obey His voice.

By speaking to us in this way, God can communicate His will to us anywhere and anytime. He can speak to us when we are in the midst of a great crowd. The secret is to cultivate a sensitivity to His voice so that nothing else is allowed to intrude upon it, nothing else to draw our attention from it, nothing else to keep us from it.

During a period of hostilities in the Middle East, large flocks were mixed together, as many shepherds had to go to war. When the war was over, however, each shepherd wanted to reclaim his sheep. The story is told of a young shepherd boy who went back to reclaim his flock.

"How many did you have?" the commanding officer asked.

"I had one hundred sheep," the boy told him.

Turning to one of his officers, the man said, "I want you to go and pick out one hundred of the best sheep in the flock and give them to this shepherd boy."

"No, sir!" the shepherd boy protested. "I don't want someone else's sheep. I want my sheep."

"But, Son," the officer said, "there are thousands of sheep out there. How are you going to tell which ones are yours?"

He said, "Oh, Sir, that's no problem. I know my sheep."

The officer was skeptical, but he was willing to learn, so he allowed the boy to enter the field where the sheep were grazing. As he walked along talking, an amazing thing happened. Most of the sheep ignored his presence, but others seemed to get very excited. One by one, particular sheep made their way from among the countless others to line up behind their shepherd and to follow him home.

The Great Shepherd is speaking to His sheep in these last days, showing us things that will amaze us as we get closer to His arrival on the scene. Hear His still, small voice.

CHAPTER TEN

THROUGH DESIRE

I delight to do thy will, O my God: yea, thy law is within my heart.   Psalms 40:8

Another way in which God speaks to us is through desire. This may seem strange to some, for desire is usually connected to evil, to flesh, rather than good. With the righteous, however, that is not true. We can say with the Psalmist, *"I delight to do thy will, O my God: yea, they law is within my heart."* Our desires are no longer carnal.

To the righteous, then, God is able to speak in this very special way, by allowing us to feel His heart, by placing in us His desires. His desires, in fact, become our desires — when we love Him as we should.

This method of hearing from God would not work with carnal people. They would have no way of distinguishing between their fleshly desires and the will of God. When you love the Lord enough, however, this impediment disappears.

David received the revelation:

Hear the Voice of God

Delight thyself also in the Lord: and he shall give
thee the desires of thine heart.   Psalms 37:4

It is because you are "delight[ing]" yourself in the Lord that He is able to give you *"the desires of [your] heart."* These are clearly not carnal or selfish desires. This promise is for those who feel God's heart.

If you love the Lord with all you heart and you suddenly have a strong desire that you didn't always have, God is probably trying to show you something. Respond to His urgings. Many who have these experiences question them and wonder why they are feeling this way. In the past we tried to suppress our feelings, because they were carnal. Now, however, we must give vent to our feelings, because they are divinely inspired.

This is not to say that we have already become perfect or that every thought or feeling we have is wholly righteous. How can we personally know if our desires are fleshly or divinely inspired? If, for example, we are on some mission field, and physical circumstances are difficult (we are sleeping on the floor and eating a limited amount of food in a way in which you are not accustomed to eat), it won't be long before our flesh begins to rebel and we have desires to get on the next flight out of there and go back home. It should be easy to recognize that this desire is not of God and should be resisted.

If, on the other hand, we suddenly have a desire

to go to Israel, to walk in the places where Jesus walked, to see the miracle of the land and the people, it is probably God speaking to our hearts, placing that godly desire in us. Satan would never do that.

Sometimes I feel an urgency to get up and go somewhere else. Invariably, when I respond to this feeling, I find someone who is looking for me. This has always been a rather puzzling experience for me, and one I can't totally understand or explain; but I know it is from God. I can be completely contented, doing what I am doing, and suddenly I will feel restless, almost troubled; and I am not satisfied until I obey what I am feeling. I thank God that He allows me to feel what He is feeling at that moment and to lead me in this gracious way.

Count it a great privilege when God speaks to you through desire. It indicates His trust in you and His desire to deal with you on a more mature level. Be careful not to betray His trust. Walk softly before the Lord, when this happens, because greater days are ahead for you.

Another precautionary note is necessary here. This is, perhaps, the most abused of all the methods by which God speaks. Too many spiritually immature people believe that everything they feel has to come from God and they are often terribly wrong.

We were at an all day meeting of one of our churches some years ago when one of the members told me he would not be there that night. He "felt led," he said, to preach somewhere else that night. I questioned him because he had a very large family and we had counted on them being in the service that night.

"Are you sure this is God?" I asked, "If you leave, you're taking ten or twelve people with you, and that will leave a considerable empty section in the church tonight. We'll miss you." But he felt sure that he had heard the voice of God.

When I saw him the next time, a couple of weeks later, I asked him how the service had gone. "Do you know what," he replied, sheepishly, "I got there and the church was closed that night."

Just be sure you are hearing the voice of God. Your own desires may be contrary to His.

CHAPTER ELEVEN

THROUGH MATURE BELIEVERS

> *Obey them that have the rule over you, and sub-*
> *mit yourselves: for they watch for your souls, as*
> *they that must give account, that they may do it*
> *with joy, and not with grief: for that is unprofit-*
> *able for you.*   Hebrews 13:17

God has graciously placed in the Body those who have greater spiritual insight and experience, for the benefit of all those who are less spiritually mature; and He has commanded us to submit ourselves to one another, and to help one another in knowing and fulfilling God's will in our lives. This is the very purpose for the existence of the major Christian ministries:

> *And he gave some, apostles; and some, prophets;*
> *and some, evangelists; and some, pastors and*
> *teachers; For the perfecting of the saints, for the*
> *work of the ministry, for the edifying of the body*
> *of Christ: till we all come in the unity of the faith,*
> *and of the knowledge of the Son of God, unto a*

perfect man, unto the measure of the stature of the fulness of Christ: That we henceforth be no more children, tossed to and fro, and carried about with every wind of doctrine, by the sleight of men, and cunning craftiness, whereby they lie in wait to deceive; But speaking the truth in love, may grow up into him in all things, which is the head, even Christ: From whom the whole body fitly joined together and compacted by that which every joint supplieth, according to the effectual working in the measure of every part, maketh increase of the body unto the edifying of itself in love. Ephesians 4:11-16

Mature believers have the responsibility before God of *"perfecting the saints,"* therefore we are advised to *"obey them."* This obedience is for our own good.

In the early Church, those who were more spiritually mature were known as *"elders,"* and it was these *elders* who were placed in positions of responsibility and who were given authority over the whole flock of God and the many decisions involving it.

It is a general rule in scripture that we listen to and obey those whom God has set over us in the Church. This submission, first to God, and then to His authority figures, is laid out very clearly in His

Word. The Bible teaches the obedience of children to their parents:

> *Children, obey your parents in the Lord: for this is right.* Ephesians 6:1

It teaches submission of the wife to her godly husband:

> *Wives, submit yourselves unto your own husbands, as unto the Lord.* Ephesians 5:22

And it teaches submission to those in spiritual leadership: *"Obey them that have the rule over you."* We are taught by Scripture to honor the men and women of God, as we honor God.

> *Render therefore to all their dues: tribute to whom tribute is due; custom to whom custom; fear to whom fear; honour to whom honour.*
> Romans 13:7

> *Let the elders that rule well be counted worthy of double honour, especially they who labour in the word and doctrine.* 1 Timothy 5:17

Since your pastor is responsible before God for your spiritual oversight, it is not your responsibility to overrule him — even if you feel he may be wrong. He will have to answer before God. Your duty is to obey.

If the advice of your pastor is not good, God will not judge you for it. Pastors must answer to God for any wrong counsel they have given to those under their charge. If you get in the habit of overriding the counsel of your spiritual leaders, you will soon find yourself in trouble.

God definitely speaks to us through more spiritual believers. They may not say, "Thus saith the Lord." They don't have to. Yet the advice they give us in the Spirit can be just as powerful and just as anointed as any prophecy or sermon.

Because of our immaturity, we often don't like what we are being told and tend to want to dismiss it. We use a whole host of reasoning when we do it, but any reason we use is in error.

My sister Ruth and I were very blessed in this regard that we had strong parents who had themselves been under strong leadership as they were coming up in the ministry, and who had enough years of experience and teaching that they could help us avoid many of the pitfalls in life.

I didn't always appreciate what they were telling me at the time, but, over the years, I have gained an immense appreciation for their wisdom. I thank God every day that He put us under their wise counsel.

Through Mature Believers

Although I would be very hesitant to take the advice of insincere people or worldly people, I am very careful to weigh the advice of those I consider to be spiritually mature. We must, for when we listen to godly men and women, we are hearing the voice of God through mature believers.

CHAPTER TWELVE

IN THE WAY HE CAN BEST REACH YOU

Now unto him that is able to do exceeding abundantly above all that we ask or think, according to the power that worketh in us.

Ephesians 3:20

God will speak to you the way that He can reach you the easiest. You must trust Him in this because He is *"able to do exceeding abundantly above all that we ask or think."* Because we are all different, He speaks to us, as different individuals, in different ways. He may speak to you in a totally different way than He speaks to me. Usually, He likes to speak in a variety of ways — even to the same individual. There are many reasons that He does this. One reason is that He doesn't want you to always expect to hear from Him in the same way.

The fact that Elijah looked for God in the wind, in the earthquake, and in the fire shows us an important point. We often look for God in all the wrong places. We expect Him to speak as He has done in the past. We expect Him to speak as He has to others. What God is interested in is an intimate relationship with each of us in which He can speak in the way He desires to speak, indeed that He can surprise us in the way He speaks, yet we will hear Him — because we are ever attentive to His voice.

When we get accustomed to hearing God speak to us in only one way, we often don't open ourselves to other manifestations of His presence, other methods of communication, and we miss many of the wonderful things God would show us in these days.

Some people feel that they can only hear from God if they are on their knees in prayer. Others are sure that God only speaks in their bedroom. Some people must be at the altar of the church. The truth is that God can speak to you anywhere and in any way He chooses. Let Him do it in a variety of ways.

Some people always want to sit in the same seat in the church because one day God spoke to them while they were sitting in that seat. They imagine that is the only spot where they can be blessed, and they get upset if someone else sits in their seat.

As we grow in the Lord and in the knowledge of Him, we quickly learn that He is a person and can speak to us day or night, wherever we are and whatever we happen to be doing at the time.

Sometimes God has to hit people over the head with a 2 X 4, just to get their attention. He doesn't want to have to do that, but sometimes He has no choice. Sometimes God has to throw up a brick wall in front of someone, leaving them nowhere to go, so that they will stop and listen to Him. Isn't this sad?

Let God speak to you by visions, by revelations, by dreams, through His Word, through prophecy, through an audible voice, directly to your spirit in His still, small voice, through mature individuals or any other way He chooses at the moment. He desires. You don't have to have the same experiences I have or the same experiences some other man or woman of God has. Let God reveal Himself to you in His unique ways.

God knows each of us and understands how best to reach out to us. Let Him communicate His will to each one as it pleases Him.

If what you are experiencing is new and strange to someone else, they may try to discourage you and tell you that it is not of God. But just because they haven't had the same experience doesn't mean it is not of God.

If He does *"exceeding abundantly above all that we ask or think,"* it may indeed seem very strange — even to us. But, as strange as it may seem, if it is God, let Him work in His own way! Don't limit Him and don't allow others to discourage you and put a limit on your experience. Only God has the right to limit how He will do things. Be flexible. Be pliable. Be teachable. Be open to God.

Don't try to fit yourself into other people's molds. It won't work. Let God be God. Let Him do things in His own way. Let Him deal with you as He wishes.

When God speaks to you, He may tell you some strange things which will be criticized by others. Don't worry about it. If others don't understand, that's okay. If you know you are hearing the voice of God, you have nothing to worry about. Do what God has told you to do and let the results speak for themselves.

Because of the unusual hour in which we are living, you can expect God to challenge you to do unusual things, and, in doing so, we are about to see some of the most astounding miracles we have ever witnessed. Begin hearing the voice of God in the way He can best reach you.

PART III

HINDRANCES TO HEARING THE VOICE OF GOD

CHAPTER THIRTEEN

SIN, LACK OF SPIRITUALITY

But your iniquities have separated between you and your God, and your sins have hid his face from you, that he will not hear. Isaiah 59:2

The same force that separated Adam from God still separates men from God today, and just as Adam hid from God and did not want to speak with Him, men and women shun God today so that they can continue to live as they please — without God's interference. Either they are ashamed to or unwilling to face God.

God also cannot bless sin. He hates it and is repelled by it. When sin is consistently present, God must not only stop speaking with an individual, He is forced to withdraw from them until the sin can be dealt with.

The cry God wants to hear from sinners is a cry of repentance. He longs to hear sinners asking for forgiveness, seeking His mercy. Sinners say to God, "If You will just bail me out of my difficulty this time, I will serve You," but God knows the end from the beginning and is not fooled by our empty promises. When He hears a genuine cry of repentance, He always responds. He has no problem with sin — when the sinner is repentant. This is true even of believers. He has said, concerning those who are in Christ:

> *This then is the message which we have heard of him, and declare unto you, that God is light, and in him is no darkness at all. If we say that we have fellowship with him, and walk in darkness, we lie, and do not the truth: But if we walk in the light, as he is in the light, we have fellowship one with another, and the blood of Jesus Christ his Son cleanseth us from all sin.*   1 John 5-7

After we know God's attitude toward sin, the thing we must do is recognize the sin we find in ourselves and ask God to forgive us and to help us forsake the present sin and to avoid sinning again. If we try to pretend that we are already perfect, John taught, we are just kidding ourselves:

> *If we say that we have no sin, we deceive ourselves, and the truth is not in us. If we confess our sins, he is faithful and just to forgive us our sins, and to cleanse us from all unrighteousness. If we say that we have not sinned, we make him a liar, and his word is not in us.*   1 John 1:8-10

Sin, Lack of Spirituality

The ideal for which we are all striving is perfection in God. Until we reach that goal, however, we must recognize that we fall short and continually seek the Lord's help to improve, to go ever higher in His love:

> *My little children, these things write I unto you, that ye sin not. And if any man sin, we have an advocate with the Father, Jesus Christ the righteous:*　　　　　　　　　　1 John 2:1

More serious than sin, perhaps, is a general lack of spirituality. If a believer does not seek to stay close to God, to get to know Him better, to learn of Him, to know His ways, how can he know God voice? Sin can hinder us from hearing His voice, and a lack of spirituality can hinder us even more.

CHAPTER FOURTEEN

WRONG TEACHINGS AND WRONG INFLUENCES

*For the time will come when they will not endure
sound doctrine; but after their own lusts shall they
heap to themselves teachers, having itching ears;
And they shall turn away their ears from the truth,
and shall be turned unto fables.*

2 Timothy 4:3-4

Another reason we are not hearing the voice of
God is that we have been taught that we can't or
that it is too difficult or that it is a rare experience,
not to be expected by the average believer — at least
not on a regular basis. Such teachings have stunted
the spiritual development of the Church.

For example, many people are teaching that the
only way to know God's will is through circumstances. This is a TERRIBLE teaching! Just the
opposite is usually true. God usually stands against
the prevailing circumstances, and when we do His
will it is usually through overcoming the negative
circumstances of our lives. If we all wait until the

circumstances are right before we do anything for God, we will be waiting a very long time.

Wrong teachings are propagated by people who lack spirituality and may be covering their own tracks. They are propagated by insincere people who have no interest in the truth, and they are propagated by immature people who don't know any better. Also, wrong teachings are sometimes spread by sincere people who are just honestly mistaken.

Some people have been guilty of neglecting to help others to learn to hear God's voice because they want us to believe that they are the only ones who have this privilege, the only ones good enough for it. They are absolutely mistaken and misguided.

Whatever the reason wrong teachings are given, they have the same damaging effects on those who hear them. If you tell a child over and over how dumb he is, he begins to accept it as truth and will start to act dumb. If, on the other hand, you make a child see how unique and extraordinary he is, he will blossom and produce accordingly. Children have a way of living up to their parents' expectations for them.

If you are told over and over that God doesn't speak today as He did with Adam and Eve, with the patriarchs and with Moses, you never expect it and will not take the time and make the effort to train yourself to hear God's voice. If I can convince you that you have every right to hear the voice of

Wrong Teachings and Wrong Influences

God, not just once in a while, but every day and many times a day, that frees you to start listening for Father's voice.

So the problem is not God. The problem resides in us, in our warped teachings, in our limiting traditions, in our lax expectations for ourselves and those around us. When we recognize the damage wrong teachings can do, we must each take the time to learn the truth about God's desire to communicate with His people, and then we must each teach others, so that the effects of wrong teachings can be broken.

In the same vein, wrong influences can hinder us in hearing the voice of God. Many people who seem to be good Christians make fun of dreams and visions, of "feelings" and even of prophecy. They ask:

> *"Who told you that you could do such a thing?"*
> *"Where did you get such an idea?"*
> *"Don't you know that's never been attempted before?"*
> *"What experience do you have in that area?"*
> *"What makes you think you are so much better than anyone else?"*
> *"Better people than you have tried that and failed."*
> *"What makes you think you can just go around the world on a shoestring?"*

They may be relatives, friends, or even church

members or leaders; but, whoever, they are danger-ous to your spiritual future. People who say these things may think they are doing you a great service by forcing you to be practical, to recognize your true situation, to admit your limitations; but, in reality, they are Satan's servants in that moment. You are not moving on the basis of your situation or your lack of limitations. You are moving by faith in the greatness of God who has called you and who will be with you and work with you in everything that you undertake for His glory. He is calling you to do what you cannot do. Therefore, others may not think what you are saying is possible. They are right, but you are about to do the impossible, through God's help.

Most people who serve God have someone in their family who is sure they are crazy not to live like others live. But those of us who live by faith in the Lord know it would be crazy to live any other way. Each of us must learn to turn a deaf ear to this type of statement. It is possible to continue to love those around you and continue to obey the Lord at the same time.

If people actually get abusive and begin to put you down because what you are doing is "foolish" to them, never mind. That's all part of serving God. Noah's neighbors laughed because he was building a great ark on dry land, but when the rains came, they stopped laughing. Don't be moved by the doubts and fears of others.

At times, you may have to make a decision about the company you keep. In order to cultivate a sensitivity to the voice of God, you need to be around people of like mind and like spirit. If you continually associate with people of limited vision or no vision at all, you may kill your anointing and lose what revelation God has given you. Unbelieving people have a way of talking you out of the very best things God has designed for your life. You don't need that.

Chapter Fifteen

Not Really Wanting to Hear

The Lord God hath given me the tongue of the learned, that I should know how to speak a word in season to him that is weary: he wakeneth morning by morning, he wakeneth mine ear to hear as the learned. The Lord God hath opened mine ear, and I was not rebellious, neither turned away back.

Isaiah 50:4-5

I am convinced that the greatest hindrance to hearing the voice of God is not other people or the wrong teachings of the past, but our unwillingness to be obedient to God. You may not think I am right on this point. Many people don't. They are convinced that it is just too hard to hear the voice of God, that only super-spiritual people have this ability. But I have known many people down through the years who pretended to want to hear God's voice, but secretly they were afraid of what He might say to them. Consequently, God was not at liberty to speak with them. He already knew that they weren't interested in hearing His voice and doing His will.

Those of you who are parents will understand that sometimes you get tired of telling your children something over and over. They don't seem to want to believe you or obey you, so by the time you have told them the same thing twenty-five times, you are sick and tired of telling them, and you simply stop telling them. You know that what you are saying is important and that if they don't listen to you they are going to get themselves hurt or in some sort of trouble, but if they are not listening, can you keep on telling them forever? There are limits — no matter how much you love someone. Sometimes you just have to let them get into trouble, and that seems to be the only way they can learn. You don't like it, but you have no other choice.

We are living in dangerous and complicated times. God is doing new things in new ways, and we must be in touch with His Spirit and know His timing and His methods. Yet, I believe, God gets tired of telling us the same things over and over, when we are not listening, and He lets us go our own way for a while until we stumble and fall and realize that we need Him and can't go on without Him. He said to the Church:

> *He that hath an ear, let him hear what the Spirit saith unto the church.* Revelation 2:7

This is not a message to the world. It is the Church

that has closed its ears to the voice of God. We want God to hear us when we call upon Him, but we are sometimes very slow to hear Him.

What God says to us, many times, does not seem convenient at the time. We almost wonder if God hasn't gotten confused about the timing or about the advisability of even undertaking what He is suggesting. But God knows exactly what He is doing, and you can trust Him.

My parents came to Richmond, Virginia in 1937 because God spoke to them. In the natural it seemed like a foolish thing to do. Mother was pastoring a church in Western Maryland that was doing very well, and Dad was pastoring another church nearby that was also doing well. They didn't have to worry about food. Their members kept their basement storage area well stocked. Periodically, someone would back a truck up to the house and unload coal and kindling wood into the basement, as well. That year they bought their first new car. Why would they want to leave all that? But God knows what He is doing.

It is not always easy to be obedient to the voice of God. He never seems to wait until an "appropriate time." He never seems to consider my "convenience" in the matter. When He wants to act, He wants to act — right now, and that may or may not be convenient for me. Usually, it seems to be inconvenient, but in the end, I am blessed for obeying.

Mother always laughed at herself because one night when angels came to visit her in her room, she felt, for some reason, that it just wasn't a good time. "Not tonight," she told the Lord. "Let them visit someone else tonight, and send them to me some other time." She wasn't surprised when my sister told her the next morning that angels had visited her in her room.

Mother always wondered what possessed her to say, "Not tonight, Lord," in such an important matter. But we are all like that sometimes. God's timing rarely seems to be convenient for us.

Although it does not always seem easy to obey God, it ensures that God is with us in all that we do. When we resist God's timing we are the losers. There are many people available who love God so much that they are willing to go anywhere at any time. If you are not anxious to hear His voice, He will not force Himself upon you. He will simply move on to another. Do you want to be bypassed?

If God speaks to you in the middle of the night, if He demands of you some sacrifice, if He urges you to make some trip that is not convenient for you at the time, if He tells you to perform some menial task for His glory — whatever it is that God is speaking to you to do, be obedient. You will be blessed in the doing. Then, when God sees that you are obedient to His voice, He will speak to you more often.

If you want to hear the voice of God, you can. If

you are unwilling to listen and obey, your unwillingness becomes the greatest hindrance to you hearing His voice. Some people can hear God's voice on certain subjects and not on others. On those other subjects, however, their ears are closed. They would rather do what they want to do than even know what God wants in the situation.

Some years ago, when some of our staff were preparing to make a mission trip to England, I remembered that God had spoken to a certain woman months before that she would minister in London. So, I asked her, "Are you going to London?"

She said, "The Lord hasn't told me a thing about going."

I sensed that she might not be open to going to London just at the moment, since it might not seem like a convenient time for her, so I asked, "Have you been listening? Give Him a chance to speak to you. If He doesn't want you to go right now, He'll tell you. But if this is the time, you should get ready."

She agreed to make it a serious matter of prayer and to listen to what God would say to her; and, sure enough, soon God spoke to her to go, and she went.

We don't always want to hear God's opinion on a particular subject. We don't always want to be sent to a particular place at the moment or to say or do a particular thing. So we close ourselves to what God is saying, avoiding Him, pretending we don't hear His gentle nudges.

When you have a family to take care of, it doesn't always seem logical to hear the voice of God calling you to some venture for Him. "What will happen to your family?" your flesh screams. You come to the conclusion that this can't be from God and stop listening to what God is saying on the subject.

We ignore the fact that God knows how to resolve all the problems we feel have no resolution. We ignore the fact that God knows how to supply everything that we imagine is impossible to secure. If we let Him have His way, we later wonder why we were even worried about this matter in the first place. The solution was so simple.

When you say, "Speak, Lord, for Thy servant heareth Thee," you cannot imagine where that decision will take you. God will open one door after another for you — if you listen to Him and obey Him.

The thing that hinders many and makes them reluctant to hear the voice of God is the fear of change. When John heard the voice of God, the voice seemed to signify a change of direction, and John had to turn to obey God. God often speaks of change, and we are not always ready to receive that change. We are so taken up with the direction we have been traveling that it seems wrong for us to turn. We are having so much fun doing what we have been doing for so long that we can't seem to make the shift. Consequently, we miss the new thing God is wanting to do in our lives. Change is not something we need to be afraid of.

In America we experienced great revival in the years 1948, 1949 and 1950. At the time that Israel was becoming a nation again after so many centuries, and the Jewish people were returning to the land, Americans were experiencing spiritual awakening. Large numbers of people sat and wept in God's presence as He restored to His people the gifts and manifestations of the Spirit that had been so common in the founding period of the Church. During those years, many great Christian leaders were raised up: Oral Roberts, A.A. Allen, Katherine Kuhlman, Billy Graham, T.L. Osborne, Morris Cerullo, Gordon Lindsay, W.V. Grant, Sr. and others. This revival was so intense and so widespread that it was named and thereafter called "Latter Rain."

Surprisingly, some of the existing Pentecostal churches did not accept what God was doing in the Latter Rain Revival. They said, "If this was of God, it would have come to us first." And because it had not happened in the way they expected, although they were good Spirit-filled people, they were unable or unwilling to change direction and move with the flow of God, and they were bypassed.

This same thing has happened over and over throughout the centuries. When God has been ready to do a new thing, His people have been so busy doing the old thing that they couldn't seem to hear His voice or believe that what they were hearing was from God, so they went in their old ways, while God raised up a new generation to do His will.

Nearly fifty years have gone by since the revival of "latter rain." We have gone through several other periods of intense spiritual activity, but right now the rain is falling as never before. It is revival time, time for a fresh visitation from God. Will you heed God's voice and move into the new thing He is doing? Or will you be bypassed because you are too busy to hear His voice?

Some people seem to have their fingers in their ears, pretending not to hear, because they are unwilling to be obedient to the voice of God. If we want to be a part of end-time revival, we must get ourselves into the place of hearing and understanding the Spirit's communications.

If you want to be on the front line of battle, if you want to be on the "cutting edge" of what God is doing, there is no substitute for hearing His voice. If you are satisfied for others to fight the major battles and win the major victories, I feel sorry for you. I want to be in the thick of the battle for the Lord. If you are more concerned with being "safe" and "sure" and "secure," if you are one of those who is determined to keep his feet "on solid ground," you will never see the miraculous power of God as He intended it to be in your life.

If you are willing to step out on the waters at His beck and call, not knowing whether or not the waters can hold you, not knowing what will take place tomorrow, not knowing whether or not you will be considered "successful" by those around you, you can be one of those who see the power of God begin to manifest itself in a new and unusual way.

Some people are terrified by the thought of doing extraordinary things. They would rather do what everyone else is doing so that no one will think they are strange. I am just the opposite. I want to do exciting things. I want to be ever enlarged and stretched. I want to continually rise to new heights and new challenges. And the only way I can accomplish that is to stay close to the Lord and listen to His voice.

When we were building our open-air Tabernacle at the camp in Ashland, Virginia, I stood one day and looked from one side to the other. It seemed enormous. *What in the world are we doing?* I asked myself. *When could we ever fill a place this large?* But only a few years had gone by when God sent Brother Schambach, and every seat was filled, and people were standing outside.

Our faith is so limited. Our insight is so limited. When we hear God speak, it raises us to new levels of faith and lets us see things as He sees them. This should be an exciting and welcome experience, not something we fear.

Some years ago I met a young minister here in our state who had been in the ministry only a few years but who was running over a thousand in his church. He didn't know that what he was doing was unusual. He didn't know that you aren't supposed to do things like that so young. The only thing he knew was that he had heard the voice of God and responded to that voice; and God had done the work for him.

God may speak to you the most unusual things, but the end result will be glorious if you just accept the fact that He knows what He is doing and you follow Him carefully. Just as you heard Him tell you what to do, follow Him carefully each step of the process. You don't need to know how to do it before you begin. Just follow His step-by-step instructions.

When the Lord impressed upon us to buy a radio station near us, we could have complained, "Lord, what do we know about operating a radio station?" Instead, we just obeyed, and He taught us day by day. He is the Master of the Airwaves.

Don't be scandalized when the Spirit of God speaks to you. Open yourself to what He is saying, and He will make you to understand it, along with the hows and the whys. He has great plans in store for you, greater things than you could ever dream of or imagine, but you will never even glimpse them unless you get serious about recognizing His voice and moving in obedience to Him when He speaks.

God's Spirit is constantly searching for men and women who are willing to lay their lives down for the will of their Master. He is searching for those who not only hear His voice, but respond favorably. "Yes, Lord! Yes! Yes! Yes, I will! Yes, I will! Yes, I will! Yes, I will."

Sometimes we draw back from what God is saying because we cannot comprehend it. Often, when God speaks to us, it is usually of things that are greater than we can presently contemplate. Our flesh limits our vision. We usually come to grips, little by little, with what is happening spiritually to us, and it is not difficult for us to believe for things that on the same faith level. Often, however, when God speaks, what He is saying is from a higher level, from a higher revelation, from a higher understanding. His words, therefore, often seem unusual or even ridiculous to us; and, in the natural, we cannot comprehend what He is saying or how it might come to pass.

Even the disciples of Jesus were often frightened by His revelations, and He had to tell them not to be afraid. In these critical moments, rather than back away and pretend that we don't know what God is saying, we need to fall on His mercy, tell Him that we are weak and cannot continue without His help.

Pray, "God, I need you today more than I have ever needed You before," and you will be thrilled with His response. Your recognition of weakness will not anger God in the least. He will not think any less of you for it. He will come to your rescue and lift you up into new heights of His glory.

PART IV

HEARING THE VOICE OF GOD AND HOW IT AFFEFCTS THE MINISTRY

CHAPTER SIXTEEN

HEARING
AND THE GIFT OF PROPHECY

*Go thou near, and hear all that the Lord our God
shall say: and speak thou unto us all that the Lord
our God shall speak unto thee; and we will hear
it, and do it.* Deuteronomy 5:27

Nothing could be more clear. This verse is practically a definition of a prophet. A prophet hears what the Lord says and repeats to the people what he has heard — nothing more and nothing less. A prophet cannot prophesy what he has been thinking or what he has been reading. He cannot prophesy the evening news headlines or the conventional wisdom of the moment. A prophet speaks God's words.

When we lack the ability to hear the voice of God, therefore, we automatically disqualify ourselves from the ministry of the prophet, one of the very important ministries of the end times. How can we repeat God's words to others if we cannot first hear them for ourselves? It is impossible to be a prophet if you cannot hear God's voice. If you cannot discern what the Spirit of God is saying, don't try to give advice to others in God's name.

Just before Jesus comes, just before the Church age comes to a close, God wants to bring us into the greatest realm of revelation that has existed since the period of the founding of the Church. This requires that we have sensitive ears and hear even the slightest whisper of the Lord.

During Old Testament days, prophets were often called "seers," and that was because they saw something. They were in constant contact with God, and He gave them spiritual vision and spiritual perception. They could look into existing situations and even into the future and declare what they saw.

Samuel was one of those seers. One day when he was alone with God, the Lord showed him that He would send a young man his way, a young man whom he should anoint to be the king over Israel:

> *To morrow about this time I will send thee a man out of the land of Benjamin, and thou shalt anoint him to be captain over my people Israel, that he may save my people out of the hand of the Philistines: for I have looked upon my people, because their cry is come unto me.* **1 Samuel 9:16**

This was a serious matter. A nation needed deliverance, and God was raising up a man to deliver them. But someone had to hear the voice of God and respond. Someone had to anoint the new king. Someone had to understand what God was doing.

The Bible is filled with such examples. God needs a people of keen perception who can do His bidding in the whole earth, a people who can hear what the Spirit is revealing.

My father was just such a man. Many times, as he was riding down the road in the car, on his way to a service, God would be showing him something. Later, he would bring that revelation to the attention of the whole church. Many wondered how he knew these things. He had no way of knowing them — in the natural. He was hearing the voice of God, and that gave him a prophetic edge in his ministry.

King Ahab got so upset because every time he took his soldiers down one path, the armies of Israel had moved; and he couldn't understand how they were outflanking him. He became convinced that there was a spy in his very bed chamber who was revealing his intentions to his enemies. His aides informed him, however, that it was the prophet Elijah who was revealing his secrets. The Spirit of God was showing Elijah the treachery of the enemy, and he was revealing it to those who could save the lives of the people of Israel. This is exactly what we need today.

God doesn't want His people to be ensnared in the enemy's traps. He doesn't want us always to be picking ourselves up from the ground after we have already fallen. He would rather show us the things that could make us stumble ahead of time so that we can avoid falling. God wants a prepared people. We must not wait until situations become impossible. We must believe for the Holy Ghost to reveal situations to us before they get that serious. Hear the voice of God and become a prophet in your time.

Although there is much more to be said on this subject, we have covered it in our book *The Power of Prophecy* and will not repeat it here.

CHAPTER SEVENTEEN

HEARING
AND FAITH FOR FINANCES

*Now the just shall live by faith: but if any man
draw back, my soul shall have no pleasure in him.*
Hebrews 10:38

Often the difference between those who get things
accomplished in Christian ministry and those who
don't rests in the area of finances. Those who have
faith for finances often have their own ministry and
many other people working with them, while those
who never develop faith for finances must work
under the supervision of another. Moreover, the type
of faith that permits you to move ahead, trusting
God to supply every need is not always easy to con-
vey to others.

First, this faith for finances is based on a very personal relationship with God, a relationship that is
nontransferable. Each person must develop his or
her own relationship with God.

Secondly, faith for finances depends TOTALLY on
being able to hear the voice of God. This is because

the life of faith is not just faith to do something. It is faith that when we do what God is telling us to do, He will support us. How can He not support us?

When we were building our camp Tabernacle, we needed some long lumber that was not available in many places and extremely expensive in others. God spoke to me and said, "Go look in the phone book and call Portsmouth."

I thought, *Call Portsmouth? That's a hundred miles away! We don't have listings for Portsmouth in our phone book.*

When I picked up the phone book and looked under lumber, there was a company listed with a Portsmouth address. I called the number and found that they were wholesalers who took the lumber right off the ships and resold it to retailers. "I'm sorry," the man said, "I can't help you. We cannot sell directly to the end user."

Even as he was saying that, I was wondering why God had told me to call this company if they couldn't help us, so I kept talking to the man, believing God to get hold of his heart.

"I have a forklift right here on the site," I told him. "We could unload a tractor-trailer in just a few minutes time and not hold your men up." It took some convincing, but that company finally sold us the lumber we needed, and we saved a large amount of money just on that one truckload of lumber.

This experience has been repeated over and over

through the years. Faith and obedience go together and faith for finances and obedience to the voice of God also cannot be separated.

In 1973 God spoke to me to take my mother and go to the 11th World Pentecostal Conference in Seoul, Korea. The tickets alone would cost us $1,100, and we had no money, but we booked our passage on the strength of what God had said. I wrote to Korea and made reservations for the two of us. Two days before flight time, somebody came knocking at the door, saying that God had spoken to them to bring us a check. It was for $2,000. If I had not booked the tickets in advance, it would have been too late. If I had not written to Korea and made our reservations by faith, it would have been too late. Many people have good ministries, but because they fail to hear the voice of God and move out by faith, they miss the very important things God is doing in the earth.

Some ask why God seem to always do things at the last minute. I believe it is because it makes us totally dependent upon Him, and He gets all the glory for what is accomplished. It is impossible for us to take the credit.

If God tells you to take a trip around the world, the fact that air fares have risen in recent years and a trip around the world may cost you $3,000 to $4,000, doesn't matter. What matters is what God has said to you. If you obey, He will sustain you, supplying your every need, as He has promised:

Hear the Voice of God

But my God shall supply all your need according to his riches in glory by Christ Jesus.

Philippians 4:19

When God has spoken to you and revealed His will, it doesn't matter if conditions are contrary, that times are difficult, or that everything seems to work against you. You will go forward and you will be successful, because God cannot fail.

When you have heard from God, it is easier to speak faith and harder to speak doubt. It is easier to speak faith and harder to speak fear. It doesn't make any difference how dark the situation might be. There is always an answer in Jesus, our miracle-working God.

When God has spoken, you move forward fearlessly, knowing that in His time, He will provide whatever resources are needed to get the job done. This is an important lesson for all of us, not just for those who are in ministry. God is interested in your business. He's interested in your bank account. He's interested in your prosperity. He's interested in you making the best business deal that you can make. He's interested in your financial situation being improved overnight. He's interested in every area of our lives. Being a Christian believer and being filled with the Holy Ghost is not just for church. It's for twenty-four hours a day. Before you make any business deal, get in touch with God and find out if that's what He wants you to do. Know that He wants you to be financially successful and will help you to achieve that success.

God wants to speak to you concerning every area of your life and He will — as you learn to listen.

CHAPTER EIGHTEEN

HEARING
AND THE MISSIONARY VISION

Go ye therefore, and teach all nations ... .
Matthew 28:19

Go ye into all the world, and preach the gospel to every creature. Mark 16:15

The missionary vision is the most exciting call anyone can receive. When God places His confidence in us and sends us to any part of the world to do His bidding, nothing could be more thrilling. If God is calling you, your life, one that may well have been filled with monotony and drudgery in the past, is about to be turned upside down. You are about to make some exciting changes.

Traveling to the nations and ministering to hungry souls everywhere is indeed a rare privilege, but how could anyone expect to meet the challenges of the missionary life without being able to hear the voice of God clearly? How can you work for Him if you cannot know His wishes? How can you be part of His army if you cannot hear His orders?

When people come to our camp in Virginia, they hear the testimony of many who travel for the Lord on a regular basis. Some may think, *Wow! I wish I could travel like that.* Well, I believe they can. In fact, I believe that they are commanded to travel for the Lord. Jesus said that we should go into all the world and preach the Gospel to every creature. So travel is not a luxury for the few. It is the responsibility of every member of the Body of Christ.

Traveling, however, can get very complicated. Where do you go? When? With who? The ministry of the end times, carrying the Gospel into every corner of the earth, is possible only to those who have an ear for hearing the guidance offered by our Lord. Since only He knows where you are needed today, how to get there and what to do once you get there, trying to do this work without having constant contact with Him would be ludicrous.

Traveling costs money, but money for missionary traveling is not the issue. When God calls us, He provides for us. When we are attuned to His Spirit, He not only makes known to us the hows and whys of what we are to do, but He makes the accomplishing of it easy in a financial sense.

He is ready to open every door and to give you what you need to go through that door — when you are ready to hear His voice.

Hearing and the Missionary Vision

God has given us a wonderful staff of dedicated people at our campground in Ashland, Virginia. I am so proud of them. They can preach, prophesy, and minister to the sick, but they also scrub or vacuum the floors, make the beds, cook, check people in — and anything else that needs to be done. They work long hours, are sacrificial, and still are able to travel all over the world when we aren't having activities at the camp. And not one of them receives a salary. It is because they have learned to hear the voice of God. This has opened to them new doors of ministry and enabled them to do most anything they set their hearts on.

If you can hear God's voice, He can let you hear the Macedonian call, as did Paul, and can send you to minister to the hungry hearts in your Macedonia. He can give you a vision, as He did to Peter on the housetop and show you the new thing He is about to do in your Caesarea. He can give you a desire to pass by a certain place as He did when Jesus said, "I must needs go by way of Samaria." God knows that some hungry soul is desperate for answers in your Samaria.

Hearing the voice of God can also make you a missionary right where you are. God might tell you to stop your car in a busy place, get out, and conduct a street meeting — just when someone is passing by who desperately needs to hear about God's love. Obey the Lord. You will be blessed.

Be willing to go where God sends you and to minister to one person or to one hundred or to one thousand. Be willing to do the big jobs and the small jobs. When you think you are doing a small job, you may be surprised to see a big result.

Not everyone can be behind the pulpit; but God needs many others, those who can be His force in prayer, tearing down the strongholds of Satan, for example. Homes need prayer. Marriages need put back together. Drug addicts need to be delivered. Some little one needs to be fed. Don't limit yourself to the pulpit. Let God use you wherever He desires.

When we can hear God and know clearly what He wants us to do, we can be moved with a power and authority that we have never before experienced. It is this power that our desperate world needs today.

CHAPTER NINETEEN

HEARING
AND BEING A WATCHMAN

*For thus hath the Lord said unto me, Go, set a
watchman, let him declare what he seeth.*

Isaiah 21:6

*Son of man, I have made thee a watchman unto
the house of Israel: therefore hear the word at my
mouth, and give them warning from me. When I
say unto the wicked, Thou shalt surely die; and
thou givest him not warning, nor speakest to warn
the wicked from his wicked way, to save his life;
the same wicked man shall die in his iniquity; but
his blood will I require at thine hand.*

*Yet if thou warn the wicked, and he turn not from
his wickedness, nor from his wicked way, he shall
die in his iniquity; but thou hast delivered thy soul.
Again, When a righteous man doth turn from his
righteousness, and commit iniquity, and I lay a
stumblingblock before him, he shall die: because
thou hast not given him warning, he shall die in
his sin, and his righteousness which he hath done*

shall not be remembered; but his blood will I require at thine hand.

Nevertheless if thou warn the righteous man, that the righteous sin not, and he doth not sin, he shall surely live, because he is warned; also thou hast delivered thy soul.   Ezekiel 3:17-21

God has called us as watchmen in the Body of Christ and has placed a very great responsibility upon each of us. We are called to be those who sense impending danger and who warn others. In order to fulfill this high calling, we must develop keen senses and must maintain a level of alertness much higher than the average believer. This is a serious matter. God has said that if we fail to warn the wicked and they die in their sins, their blood will be required at our hands.

How can we be watchmen if we lack the ability to sense impending dangers? How can we warn others if we don't know what is happening ourselves? We must see something and declare what we see. We must hear something and declare what we hear. This is the responsibility of the watchman.

Watchmen, start looking around. Watchmen, start listening for approaching danger. Watchmen, get your ears open to what God is saying.

Many members of the Body of Christ never worry because they know there are others who are sensitive in the Spirit. They trust these "others" to sound a warning when any danger exists. But always trusting others can be very dangerous. People change. People fail. People are not perfect.

It is not uncommon for those who fail their responsibility in the Church and even begin to speak forth their own heart rather than the will of God to take many others with them — all because people get too lax and don't seek God the way they should. As they look back later, they realize they should have seen the danger signs. They should have sensed that all was not well. They should have understood that the person they were following took a detour, but at the moment they were totally oblivious to danger. This is a tragedy that we cannot allow to happen to us.

Because we are living in the closing days of time, there are more false spirits at work than ever before. The spirit of deception, the spirit of Antichrist, is at work in the hearts of men. We cannot let down our guard. We cannot close our ears to the voice of God. It is far too dangerous.

The Word of God warns us of the apostasy of the end times:

Let no man deceive you by any means: for that day shall not come, except there come a falling away first, and that man of sin be revealed, the son of perdition; 2 Thessalonians 2:3

None of us is immune to the attacks of the enemy. Therefore, each of us must be alert to danger and ready to warn others. If you will listen to God, He will help you to recognize trouble before it overcomes you. If you will heed His warnings, He will help you to learn to recognize temptation before it overpowers you. He will show you deception before it entraps you.

You cannot afford to let down the barriers in your life. You cannot afford to give Satan free access. You cannot allow the enemy to have free rein.

We, as ministers of the Gospel, have a far greater responsibility than most. We are responsible before God for the people who stand in our pulpits and for the message they deliver. We will answer to God for allowing wolves to come in and plunder our flocks.

Ministries that were good last year are not necessarily good today. When a man is standing in your pulpit, declaring false doctrine, that is not the time to recognize the error of inviting him. You must sense ahead of time who will bless your people, who will add blessing to your church, who will come with a fresh word from Heaven.

Trying to counter erroneous teaching after a visiting minister has gone is usually too late. The damage has already been done. Don't let wolves come into your sheep pen. Don't let insincere people poison your little ones.

Hearing and Being a Watchman

Being a watchman is a double duty. When God speaks to us, we must be bold enough to declare what He is saying. It is not enough to see what He is showing us or hear what He is telling us. We must warn others of what we see and what we hear.

When you hear the voice of God, there is much that you no longer want to be identified with. It is no longer acceptable to you just to turn your head and ignore what is going on. It is no longer acceptable just to keep quiet about wrongdoing. You feel compelled to change your associations and change your identifications.

If you are a selfish person, forget about the ministry of watchman. This ministry demands maturity and self-denial. Some of those who have a great desire to hear the voice of God, just want to do it for personal reasons. They don't want to get involved in helping others. They don't want to make the personal sacrifices necessary to warn anyone. They want to hear, but they want to hear only for themselves, not for others.

God said to Moses:

And the Lord said, I have surely seen the afflic-
tion of my people which are in Egypt, and have
heard their cry by reason of their taskmasters; for
I know their sorrows; And I am come down to
deliver them out of the hand of the Egyptians, and
to bring them up out of that land unto a good land

and a large, unto a land flowing with milk and honey; unto the place of the Canaanites, and the Hittites, and the Amorites, and the Perizzites, and the Hivites, and the Jebusites. Now therefore, behold, the cry of the children of Israel is come unto me: and I have also seen the oppression wherewith the Egyptians oppress them. Come now therefore, and I will send thee unto Pharaoh, that thou mayest bring forth my people the children of Israel out of Egypt.   Exodus 3:7-10

Moses was not sure he wanted to get involved. After all, hadn't the Hebrews rejected him once when he had a desire to do something for them? Anyway, he considered himself to be unqualified for the task:

And Moses said unto God, Who am I, that I should go unto Pharaoh, and that I should bring forth the children of Israel out of Egypt?
                                              Exodus 3:11

Although God assured Moses that He would be with him and would help him at every turn, Moses continued to show reticence to speak to Pharaoh. In the end, God chose Aaron to speak in Moses' place. Moses was the inspiration, and Aaron was the mouthpiece. Never be reluctant to speak, to warn a sinful and adulterous generation that the coming of

Hearing and Being a Watchman

Jesus is drawing ever nearer. Never sit idly by and watch a brother fall into sin:

> *Brethren, if a man be overtaken in a fault, ye which are spiritual, restore such an one in the spirit of meekness; considering thyself, lest thou also be tempted.* Galatians 6:1

Don't just sit back and let it happen. Do something! Help your brothers! Don't just let them keep doing the things that are harmful to their spirits! Intervene! Restore them.

It is not easy to be a watchman, and many don't want to see danger approaching. They are afraid that their intervention will be resented, and they might be right. But that doesn't change our responsibility. You cannot just let things pass. God is requiring of us that we take corrective action concerning things that are not pleasing to Him.

If you were a lifeguard and you failed to warn people when they were getting out too deep or getting out into dangerous waters, what would people think of you? Yes, I know that many people may resent your warnings, feeling that you are taking all the fun out of life. They may not understand that you are protecting their very lives. If you are a lifeguard, however, that is just part of your duty — whatever people may think or say.

Rise to the challenge. Hear the voice of God and warn those around you of those things to come.

Chapter Twenty

HEARING
AND SPIRITUAL LEADERSHIP

Now after the death of Moses the servant of the Lord it came to pass, that the Lord spake unto Joshua the son of Nun, Moses' minister, saying, Moses my servant is dead; now therefore arise, go over this Jordan, thou, and all this people, unto the land which I do give to them, even to the children of Israel.   Joshua 1:1-2

There shall not any man be able to stand before thee all the days of thy life: as I was with Moses, so I will be with thee: I will not fail thee, nor forsake thee.   Joshua 1:5

And the Lord said unto Joshua, This day will I begin to magnify thee in the sight of all Israel, that they may know that, as I was with Moses, so I will be with thee.   Joshua 3:7

And the children of Israel did so as Joshua commanded ... .   Joshua 4:8

Leadership demands giftedness in the realm of knowing the mind of God. People follow those who know what God is saying and respond when called upon to serve with those who have a clear goal and a clear path to that goal. This means that anyone aspiring to leadership in the Christian Church must develop the ability to hear the voice of God.

Contrary to popular thought, leadership requires much more than a charismatic personality or an organizational ability. Joshua received his orders from God, passed them along to the people, and the people obeyed him. This is Christian leadership. I am greatly indebted to my father in this regard:

When I got saved, there was a woman living in Redbluff, California, who had a great prophetic ministry. She attended the Full Gospel Businessmen's meeting in Seattle, Washington, where I gave my heart to the Lord, and was there praying for me when Jesus got hold of my life and filled me with His Spirit. She had not really wanted to go to the meeting and had been arguing with God all week about it. Finally, she said to God, "I don't want to go, but if there will be someone there that I need to help, I'm willing. If that is the case, You will have to tell someone to call me and offer to pay my airfare, because I don't have money to go."

Within an hour, Harold Bredeson, a Spirit-filled Dutch Reformed minister, called to say, "Pastor, there is a ticket waiting for you at the airport."

Hearing and Spiritual Leadership

And so she went, and, through her ministry to me there in Seattle, became like a spiritual mother to me. The woman never had any children of her own, and this was God's way of compensating her. People called her from all over the world because she had such an open ear to God that she could hear His voice and know His will — for ministers, for businesses, and for personal lives.

I personally called her several times in those early days of my Christian experience. Sometimes I could sense from her voice that she was tired. I knew her habit of praying a good part of the night. A miracle never failed to happen, however, as I spoke with her. Suddenly her voice would change, as the anointing came upon her, and she would start to prophesy.

My purpose in calling her had not been to get a particular prophecy. Since she had been a blessing to me in those early days, I just enjoyed talking with her and found her experiences challenging. One day, however, my father said to me, "Son, it's wonderful that you can have contact with that sister and that God can use her to encourage you, but don't ever get to the place that you need somebody else to hear the voice of God for you."

That turned out to be one of the best things my father ever taught me. If I had become dependent on someone else to hear the voice of God for my life, I could never have grown into a leadership position.

In reality, each of us needs to hear God for our-selves. While it is wonderful to have fellowship with other believers and wonderful to have God use them to reveal His will to us, there is no substitute for my hearing the voice of God for myself.

There was a wonderful story told of the early days of Morse Code communications in America. Two men were sitting outside a public office waiting to be interviewed for a job. The place seemed to be de-serted. No one came out to greet them, and all they could hear were the dots and dashes of Morse Code from a telegraph terminal.

After a while a third man arrived and joined them in their wait. Before long, however, he jumped up and ran inside. The two men shouted after him, "We were here first. Wait your turn."

"I'm not waiting for anything," he answered. "This machine keeps saying, 'IF YOU CAN UNDER-STAND THIS, COME ON IN.' " The same message had been repeated over and over, and the two men who had now been waiting more than half an hour, could have gone in and gotten the job, but they couldn't hear what was being communicated, so they didn't qualify for the job.

This is why the Lord has said, *"He that hath an ear, let him hear what the Spirit is speaking."* For the normal believer it is important, but for those called to leadership, it is essential.

The people of God that we can name as having

been great ministers all had the ability to hear the voice of God:

Some years ago I was in one of Katherine Kuhlman's services at the Shrine Auditorium in Los Angeles. In that service, she didn't take time to lay hands on anyone; yet she had such a strong word of knowledge that great miracles were done in the name of the Lord.

"Someone over on this side is being healed of muscular dystrophy," she would say.

"Someone else is being healed right now of cirrhosis of the liver."

"Someone over here is being healed of cancer." And it was so.

People were healed by the hundreds in those meetings — as the word of the Lord came forth out of her mouth. She was hearing from God, and that is what made her great.

William Branham had probably the greatest word of knowledge ministry of his generation. In the early days of his ministry he would see colors on his wrist which would indicate to him something about the sickness the person standing before him had. He did not know them and had asked them no questions in this regard, but would properly diagnose their condition — through the Spirit. Each time the person would confirm that he had diagnosed their condition correctly.

Later God used him in another way. He always

came onto the platform very meekly and quietly, and stood there talking in a normal conversational voice for a time. He would say, "I'm waiting for the angel." After five or six minutes, a great change would come in his demeanor and in his voice, and nobody had to tell you when the angel came. Before long, he began calling out the names of individuals who were present, giving their complete addresses, their telephone numbers and other detailed pertinent information. He would tell each individual what exactly was wrong with them and why they had come seeking his prayers.

He told one woman that she was Jewish, that she should not have come to the meeting (by her own religious standards), but that she had come (on a Greyhound bus) because her husband was home in Chicago, dying and she had heard about this ministry. He told her name and her address in detail. Then he asked her, "Do you believe I am a prophet of the Lord?" When she replied that she did, he told her to go home, and she would find her husband completely healed. When he told these things in such detail great faith was created and the results were always wonderful. People came from everywhere to hear him—because he was hearing from Heaven.

Similar miracles were done through the ministry of A.A. Allen. He would begin to describe a vision he was having, convinced that it was for someone in the audience. Every time he did this, someone would receive a wonderful miracle.

Hearing and Spiritual Leadership

Brother R.W. Schambach, who was a coworker of Brother Allen's, describes what happened one night as "one of the greatest miracles [he] had ever seen." Before the service he had spoken to a woman he had noticed in the crowd for the past five or six nights. She had something in a large basket she always placed on the front row. When he went near, he could not believe what he saw in that basket. It was a child, already five or six years old, but never properly developed. He was like a vegetable.

He had no genitals, and had, in all, twenty-six debilitating conditions. Doctors had been amazed that he even survived a few months, but that mother's prayers had kept her son alive for many years, and she was now desperate for a greater miracle for him. She had told Brother Schambach, "I have only twenty dollars left. I will have to go back home tonight after the service, so I am believing God to do something for my son tonight."

During the course of the service, Brother Allen took up an offering, challenging the people to make sacrifices in their giving. Brother Schambach watched in amazement as the woman he had spoken to earlier got up, went forward, and placed her only remaining bill in the offering bucket. He knew that she now had no gas money to get home and that God would surely do a special miracle for her before the night was over.

Later in the service, Brother Allen began to have a vision. He described a delivery room and the birth of a child. The child, he said, was deformed. He described ten or twelve different physical problems the child had and, toward the end of his vision, declared in a loud voice, "That child is being healed! Whoever has that child, bring him to the platform." As everyone watched in amazement, that deformed lump began to move and to get to its feet and to be healed. After all his years of successful ministry, Brother Schambach still tells that story with awe at what God did that night.

Well, if God worked that way through Katherine Kuhlman and God worked that way through William Branham and God worked that way through A. A. Allen, He can still work that way today. He has not changed. He is waiting for those who can hear His voice.

Hearing the voice of God for yourself is the greatest experience you could ever have in this world. It does something for you that no other experience can do. When it happens, suddenly you can travel to China, to Russia, or to the islands of the sea. You can go anywhere in the world without fear, because God is everywhere, and you know that His Spirit will be faithful to speak to you and guide you — wherever you happen to be at the moment.

Hearing the voice of God, therefore, not only becomes a blessing to your personal life, it sets you up for a leadership position in the Church of the Lord Jesus Christ.

PART V

DEVELOPING A SENSITIVITY TO THE VOICE OF GOD

CHAPTER TWENTY-ONE

THE IMPORTANCE OF PRAYER AND FASTING

So we fasted and besought our God for this: and he was intreated of us. Ezra 8:23

I humbled my soul with fasting; and my prayer returned into mine own bosom. Psalms 35:13

I have never been able to teach hearing the voice of God without also teaching fasting, for the two are inextricably linked in my mind. One of our tape series that has been such a blessing to many people through the years is entitled, *Fasting and Prayer and Hearing the Voice of God.* These two subjects go together. Since fasting is such a detailed subject, I have chosen to address it in a separate volume and to concentrate, here, on the subject at hand. I cannot however, publish a book about hearing the voice of God that doesn't say something about fasting.

I have learned over the years that if we can begin to fast and pray and hear the voice of God, we can go anywhere and do anything for the Lord. That message has not diminished in importance with time, for there has never been a more critical time in the history of the Church than NOW. We need to learn to fast and pray effectively NOW.

Although fasting blesses us in many ways, both spiritual and physical, nothing helps to sharpen our spiritual perception like fasting and prayer. NOTHING! If Moses fasted, and Daniel fasted, and Paul fasted and Jesus fasted, you and I need to fast too. In fact, regular fasting and prayer is the very first habit we need to develop in order to cultivate a hearing ear.

What fasting does may be somewhat of a mystery. It seems to be nothing more than a physical act, but it is an act of obedience, and it is an act of self-denial. When we tell God that we are willing to deny our flesh the right to food for a determined period it does much to shift the balance of power in our lives from the natural to the supernatural. When we close ourselves in with God in fasting and prayer, we loose the forces necessary to spiritual guidance. And somehow we become more sensitive to the Lord's voice.

Fasting, although it is a wonderful blessing in its own right, is combined in the Scriptures with prayer. It is not enough to deny the flesh the natural food. We must get into God's presence and feast on the supernatural.

As you learn the importance of talking with God

The Importance of Prayer and Fasting

on a regular basis (prayer is nothing more than fellowship and communion with God), you will begin to reap the benefits of His presence. David said:

Thou wilt shew me the path of life: in thy presence is fulness of joy; at thy right hand there are pleasures for evermore.   Psalms 16:11

Just one of those many benefits is the ability to recognize His voice. Taking specific time for that communion also lets God know that you are serious and gives Him the opportunity He needs to reveal Himself to you. When you take time to commune with Him, He speaks to you and ministers to your every need.

I love to walk when I pray, and the greater I feel the anointing, the faster I walk. Sometimes I feel like running. What I do not do is concentrate on problems as I pray. I concentrate on talking to God and attempt to forget the problem. The problem is not the important thing. The important thing is maintaining proper contact with the Problem Solver.

Often, when I need an urgent answer to prayer, I get so taken up in my prayer that I forget about the need I wanted to pray about. It is only later that it comes back to me, and I realize that I forgot all about it. But God still supplies my every need — whether I remember to ask Him for it or not.

The important thing for me to do in prayer is to

tell the Lord how much I love Him, how much I appreciate Him, and how great and mighty He is. Worshiping Him is much more important than presenting our wish lists. That doesn't mean that I won't receive what I need from the Lord. As I forget my need and begin to love and worship Him, the Holy Ghost drops the answer to my problem into my spirit when I am least expecting it. Later, I wonder why I ever worried about that matter and what took me so long to get my answer.

It is wonderful to get other people praying for you. It is wonderful to partners, those who share needs together in prayer. But, in the end, no one can do anything at all to further the personal relationship you enjoy with the Lord except YOU. It's just you and Him. Make the sacrifice. It's worth it. Set aside time for fasting and prayer and communion with God. Learn to know His voice.

CHAPTER TWENTY-TWO

WALKING SOFTLY BEFORE THE LORD

*While it is said, To day if ye will hear his voice,
harden not your hearts, as in the provocation.*
Hebrews 3:15

*Again, he limiteth a certain day, saying in David,
To day, after so long a time; as it is said, To day if
ye will hear his voice, harden not your hearts.*
Hebrews 4:7

Besides our prayer life, there is much that we can
do to cultivate an intimate, personal relationship
with the Lord. We can learn to love what He loves
and hate what He hates, to walk softly before Him.

In every way we must try to live a life pleasing to
God. Anything that the devil can use against us, to
hinder our prayer life and to hinder the clarity with
which we hear the Lord, he will not hesitate to use
it. We must learn, little by little, the things in our
lives that are not convenient to our spiritual growth
and prosperity and forsake them. In this way, we
are constantly confirming to God that we are on His

side and, just as important, confirming to the devil, that we have left his ways — permanently.

Satan will not volunteer to leave you alone and will continually insist that you return to your old life. In these moments, you must take authority over him and send him on his way. He has no right to torment you like this. The Bible teaches us to not *"give place"* to the devil:

Neither give place to the devil.   Ephesians 4:27

That means don't give him an opportunity. Don't start feeling lonesome and sorry for yourself and allow Satan to come and sit on your shoulder and whisper in your ear. Instead, we are to *"resist the devil,"* and when we do resist him, we are promised, *"he will flee"*:

Submit yourselves therefore to God. Resist the devil, and he will flee from you.   James 4:7

Submitting to God and resisting the devil, then, become the double edges of our sword of victory in the Christian life. When you fail to do either, you not only put at risk your sensitivity to the voice of God, but you put at risk your very soul.

The writer of Hebrews quoted several times the Old Testament admonition, that if we want to hear God's voice, we must not allow our hearts to become hardened, as happened to many believers throughout history. The hardening of the heart doesn't happen overnight. It comes in slow increments and sometimes you almost cannot discern that it is happening at all — until it is too late.

If you notice at some point that you find no joy in prayer, if you notice that you find no joy in the reading of God's Word, if you notice that you find no joy in fellowship with other believers, count these as important danger signals and throw yourself immediately upon the mercy of God. Don't allow this condition to continue — even for a short time. It is too risky and there is too much at stake.

Ask God why. Ask Him what you have done to grieve His Spirit. Ask Him what you have said to cause Him to withdraw His presence. Repent of your failing immediately and return to the Lord's favor.

When the Lord revealed His Word for the various churches to the Apostle John, the news was not all good. To the Church at Ephesus, He said:

Nevertheless I have somewhat against thee, because thou hast left thy first love. Remember therefore from whence thou art fallen, and repent, and do the first works; or else I will come unto thee quickly, and will remove thy candlestick out of his place, except thou repent. Revelation 2:4-5

This same thing could be said of nearly every

Christian at some point in their lives. Most everyone experiences lukewarmness or loss of zeal at some point. The solution to the problem, God said, is to *"remember from whence thou art fallen"* and *"repent."* That is simple enough. If we are willing to see our failure, God is willing to restore us to His presence. If we are willing to recognize the things that keep us from hearing His voice, He is willing to continue to commune with us.

The problem with many believers is that they have lost their first love and don't even know it. Their experience has become so filled with tradition that they don't realize the spark has gone out of their relationship with God. What a shame!

You can't afford to let things go that far in your case. If you don't hear from God today, start finding out why and do something about it NOW. Don't wait. This is a life and death situation that calls for drastic measures. Your life is at stake. Act now. Push aside anything else that needs to be pushed aside. Nothing must take precedence over maintaining a healthy relationship with God. Take whatever time is necessary. Spend any amount that you need to spend. Take any action that is essential to your spiritual health. Do it without a second thought and without concern for what others may think or say. This is your soul we are talking about.

Then, let hearing the voice of God become, for you, the test of your relationship. Don't let a single day go by without hearing and recognizing His voice. Expect it. Desire it. Listen for it. And give God opportunity to do it.

With many people in our modern world, it is all a matter of time. They don't have time to hear from God. If it's not on their E-mail, on their Voice-mail or their answering machine, forget it. Their schedule is too tight. When they do have time, their life is so cluttered with other noises that God doesn't have a chance to get through to them. David's admonition is:

Be still, and know that I am God: I will be exalted among the heathen, I will be exalted in the earth.
Psalms 46:10

If we are giving God no moments of stillness, no quietness of spirit and mind, during which He can reveal His will to us, can we blame Him because the Church isn't hearing from Heaven? Some married couples have such busy schedules these days that they must make time for each other, arrange a date, as it were. If that's what it takes to hear from God, then we need to do it. We need to come aside from the activity of the day and listen to His words of comfort and direction. I will warn you, however, that God does things in His time, not yours, at His convenience, not yours, and in His way, not yours.

Learn to take advantage of any spare time you

have to cultivate your relationship with God and learn to hear His voice. While you are driving your car, while you are walking down the street or through a mall, even while you are on your job, you can let God speak to you and reveal Himself to you. Learn to walk softly before the Lord.

CHAPTER TWENTY-THREE

LEARNING THROUGH THE OFFERING

*Every man according as he purposeth in his heart,
so let him give; not grudgingly, or of necessity:
for God loveth a cheerful giver.*

2 Corinthians 9:7

This act of *"purposing"* what to give in an offering can be a very wonderful experience. In order to receive the greatest blessing possible from our giving, the "purposing" needs to be God-inspired, not just what we want to give at the moment or what seems convenient for us to give. Because of this exciting principle, we have found the offering to be a good place to start learning to hear God's voice.

This may work so well because of the increased motive involved of wanting to receive financial blessing in return. Since we all have financial needs and we all want to prosper, this is an excellent place to begin.

When an offering is taken, ask the Lord how much you should give. Then obey His voice. Two things will result: You will prosper because of your obedience to the Lord, and you will develop a hearing ear in the process.

Sometimes God may lead you to give much, and sometimes He may lead you to give little. Always giving a lot is not always His way. While it is good to be generous and better to err on the side of generosity than on the side of stinginess, obeying God's voice implicitly is the best and safest way to give.

Like everything else, most of us fall into habits in our giving. If we are accustomed to putting a bill of a certain value into the offering plate, we automatically search for a bill of that value when an offering is taken. If we are accustomed to writing a check of a certain amount, we automatically begin to write the next one for that same amount. While it is not wrong to give systematically, always giving the exact same amount without question is a bad habit to develop. Don't always give the same amount. Let the Lord lead you in your giving.

God wants giving to be exciting, spontaneous, divinely inspired and a blessing to you and to His Church. When you hear God's voice in the offering, it changes from a necessary drudgery into a glorious opportunity designed for world evangelism and your financial prosperity.

Since most churches take offerings, every time you go to church, there will probably be at least one offering, one opportunity to give. First, pay your tithes. That is not optional. Then, ask God what He would have you to give beyond the tithe, in what we call our "discretionary giving." That means it is at your discretion. Let it be, however, at God's discretion. He knows best.

God's plan for your prosperity requires your obedience in giving. He said:

> *Give, and it shall be given unto you; good measure, pressed down, and shaken together, and running over, shall men give into your bosom. For with the same measure that ye mete withal it shall be measured to you again.* Luke 6:38

We all want God to bless us, but most of us are unaware that His blessing requires that we first give. Prosperity appeals to everyone, but prosperity involves your giving in accordance with God's will. You must give the amount He desires, at the time He desires and at the place He designates.

Since your financial prosperity and the financial prosperity of your family is involved, you simply cannot afford to allow your giving to become mechanical, traditional or commonplace. "How much, God?" should always be your prayer. He may tell you to give more than you intended, or He may tell you to give less. Since He knows best, trust Him and obey.

There is another principle behind our giving through hearing the voice of God that many of us overlook. It is the principle of the proper steward-ship of everything the Father has entrusted into our hands. Jesus taught:

Blessed are those servants, whom the lord when he cometh shall find watching: verily I say unto you, that he shall gird himself, and make them to sit down to meat, and will come forth and serve them. And if he shall come in the second watch, or come in the third watch, and find them so, blessed are those servants. And this know, that if the goodman of the house had known what hour the thief would come, he would have watched, and not have suffered his house to be broken through. Be ye therefore ready also: for the Son of man cometh at an hour when ye think not. Then Peter said unto him, Lord, speakest thou this parable unto us, or even to all? And the Lord said, Who then is that faithful and wise steward, whom his lord shall make ruler over his household, to give them their portion of meat in due season? Blessed is that servant, whom his lord when he cometh shall find so doing. Of a truth I say unto you, that he will make him ruler over all that he hath.

Luke 12:37-44

All that is in my pocket belongs to God. Every-thing that I have in my bank account is His. Everything that I own came from only one Source. I am only a steward of God's riches. Everything I have in my possession is His. When He urges me to give, I know that He has my best interests at heart. Why, then, should I hesitate when He speaks to me? If He asks me to give the last $20 I have in my pocket, I always know that He has $200 waiting for me somewhere. I never lose by giving.

Your gift not only secures your own prosperity, it may be the means of bringing revival to many hungry hearts. Thank God that He allows us to be participants in the harvest, to be co-laborers with other members of the Body.

Be obedient to God not only in the giving of your money, but in other things, as well:

Some years ago God enabled me to buy an evangelistic tent from Florida. It was 60' x 120'. It was just before camptime that year, so I couldn't use it immediately, but I could hardly wait. My father instilled in me a love for tents and tent revivals.

During camptime that year, we had a preacher from Australia. He asked us all to pray for him because he needed a tent for his ministry back home. So we prayed. "Oh, God, help our brother to get a tent so that he can do a greater work for You in Australia."

As we prayed, God spoke to me and said, "Give him your tent."

I tried to ignore that word and to keep claiming another tent for my brother. "God, you know my brother needs a tent. Some way, somehow, supply his need."

Again God said, "Give him yours."

I kept praying, "Oh, God, you know my brother needs a tent. Give him a tent."

Again God said, "Give him yours."

I couldn't ignore this any longer, so I reasoned with God. "God, I haven't even opened my new tent. I haven't really even seen it, much less used it. You gave me that tent because I needed it so badly."

God said, "Give it to him!"

When I finally stopped arguing with God, I said to the people, "Well, you prayed and God answered. He told me to give our brother my tent." We then took an offering to ship the tent to Australia.

Did I lose by obeying God? Not at all. When I gave up that tent, which was a used one, God gave me a new one, bigger than the one we had shipped to Australia. I was so glad I had heard His voice.

One summer, during campmeeting, God spoke to five or six of our staff people to give their cars away. They were not trying to get out of ministry. They were believing for better vehicles to use for God, and they got them. It works.

Every steward must one day give an account of his stewardship, and each of us will one day give a full accounting to God:

> *So then every one of us shall give account of him-self to God.*   Romans 14:12

Learning Through the Offering

The final proof that giving, in itself, is not sufficient comes from the writings of the Apostle Paul to the Church at Corinth:

And though I bestow all my goods to feed the poor, and though I give my body to be burned, and have not charity, it profiteth me nothing.

1 Corinthians 13:3

Let all your giving be Divinely motivated and let the offering be an occasion for learning to hear God's voice.

CHAPTER TWENTY-FOUR

DECLARING WHAT YOU HEAR

The Lord God hath given me the tongue of the learned, that I should know how to speak a word in season to him that is weary: Isaiah 50:4

If we are interested in hearing the voice of God only for ourselves, we will surely miss a great part of what God desires to do for each of us. His highest will is to speak to you on behalf of others, to give you *"the tongue of the learned,"* so that you will know how to speak *"a word in season to him that is weary."* If you believe to hear only for yourself and your own needs, you will hear only for yourself, but if you give yourself to the desires of the heart of God, He will begin to allow you to share the burden of your fellowman.

When you have this greater vision, it is necessary to begin to declare what God is saying to you. The first step in this declaration is to boldly declare that you are hearing from God. Don't ever be ashamed to say, "The Lord told me ..."

Some people may be offend by your saying that

and will respond sarcastically, "Who do you think you are saying 'the Lord' told you ... ?" Never mind what other people say! God is your Father, and He loves you, and wants to talk to you every day. If people are offended by that fact, so be it. You must begin declaring the fact that you are hearing from God.

The next time you hear that voice of God, say, "Jesus spoke to me." "Jesus told me to call." "Jesus told me to go." "Jesus told me to do it."

It pleases Him when you give Him the glory and will cause Him to speak to you more often and to reveal Himself to you more consistently.

Stop saying, "I have a feeling," and start giving the Lord the glory He deserves. Stop saying, "Something told me to do it," and tell it like it is. God has placed His desire in us.

Some people are saying, "I was just supposed to be there at that exact time." Well, that doesn't really give Him glory. Does it? If you were "supposed" to be there, who made that determination? The lukewarm are purposely vague and politically correct. Let us not worry about what others will think about what we are saying and start giving God the glory He deserves.

The second aspect of the declaration is the message that God may be giving you for others. It may be a word of knowledge or wisdom, a prophecy or interpretation of tongues, or just a word of encouragement or an exhortation. Whatever form it takes, start giving it forth and God will give you more. He is searching for those who will not only hear His voice, but will speak what He gives them.

He may give you the message in many forms. It may come in a dream or a vision. He may speak to you, either in an audible voice or in that still, small voice. However it comes, declare boldly what God is showing you and He will work to bring it to pass.

Hearing someone say, "The Lord spoke to me," calls people's attention. They are "all ears" when you say that.

One of the most powerful testimonies in this regard is that of Sister Jane Lowder, one of our faithful coworkers. She was working as the manager of a dairy bar in North Carolina many years ago when my uncle, Dr. William A. Ward, was holding a tent meeting in her city. One night after church he and Pastor Ashby went into the dairy bar to get something to eat. When the woman came to their table, Brother Ward felt God speaking to him about her and he said, "Sister, you're going to be a missionary. You're going to travel the world for God. You're going to do great exploits. God is going to use you so that thousands will be reached for the glory of God."

Stunned, she went back to the kitchen and said to some of the staff, "See that man sitting at that table over there? He is the craziest person I have ever met in all my life! I never saw him before and he just told me that I'm going to be a missionary for God, that I'm going to travel the world for God, and that thousands of people are going to get healed and blessed in my ministry."

It was strange, indeed, but every word of what God told Dr. Ward that day has come to pass in the life of Sister Jane Lowder. So don't take lightly what God is showing you about someone else. You never know what He can do. Declare it, and leave the rest with God.

Sometimes it takes courage and maturity to step out based on what you know God is saying, when no one else seems to have heard His voice.

My Prayer For Your Hearing

We are now approaching the final days of time and being a traditional believer is not enough anymore. Being a church member is not sufficient. God has reserved Heaven's best for those who hear His voice and obey. Not everyone who names the name of Jesus will be used in end-time revival, only a select few, those who are willing and eager to listen to the voice of the Spirit and willing to do what may seem foolish to man.

Right this moment God is looking for some storm troopers, some specially trained units that He can send into various parts of the world where men and women are hungering for Him and desire to do His will. Those who qualify for this very special ministry will have to have sensitive ears. Would you like to be a part of the group?

God is raising up those who will spearhead revival in the earth. He needs a "few good men," God's Marine units, those who will be called upon to storm the beachheads and pull down the strongholds of the enemy. There will surely be a price to be paid, and there will surely be fierce battles to be won; but what a privilege it is to be part of God's elite troops!

If you are willing to heed God's call today, I want to pray for you and believe God to do a special work in your life. I want to ask Him for the miracle of a listening ear. I have often prayed this prayer, with great effect.

When I laid hands on an Australian brother and prayed for him, he testified the next night: "I have been trying to get an answer from God for three months. I couldn't hear the voice of God. When Brother Heflin laid his hands on my ears last night, it was like God gave me another ear. He gave me a spiritual ear. Last night the Lord spoke to me and told me the things that I needed to hear."

Let God touch YOUR ears today. Let Him give you a sensitivity in the Spirit. Let Him give you a new understanding. Believe to hear His voice and to know when it is God speaking to you. Believe to know and understand His will. Pray with me:

Dear God,

In the name of Jesus, I believe You for Your people today. Many are desirous of hearing Your voice, of knowing Your will, Your plan and Your purposes. God, each of us needs direction. Speak to them, Lord. Reveal Yourself to them. Let ears be open to You. Speak to this people by day and by night, as only you can; and let them be sensitive enough to hear Your voice and be willing to obey.

My Prayer For Your Hearing

Let there be hearing!

Let there be an understanding!

Let there be knowing!

I take authority over doubt and unbelief. I take authority over confusion. I take authority over uncertainty.

Let there be clarity!

Let there be sensitivity!

I believe You for it, oh God.

> *In the Name of Jesus,*
> *Amen!*

Now worship God and receive His touch. Let Him have His way in your life through hearing His voice and obeying Him fully.

The Lord God hath given me the tongue of the learned, that I should know how to speak a word in season to him that is weary: he wakeneth morning by morning, he wakeneth mine ear to hear as the learned. The Lord God hath opened mine ear, and I was not rebellious, neither turned away back.

Isaiah 50:4-5